Jesus Christ in the Synoptic Gospels

SISTER AUDREY csc

Jesus Christ in the Synoptic Gospels

SCM PRESS LTD

334 00776 3

First published 1972
by SCM Press Ltd
58 Bloomsbury Street, London
Fifth impression 1980
Printed in Great Britain by
Richard Clay (The Chaucer Press) Ltd
Bungay, Suffolk

Contents

PART ONE

I *Background*

1. *Geography*

Jesus lived and died in Palestine. Although a small country only 150 miles in length and approximately 50 miles wide, about the size of Wales and smaller than Tasmania, Palestine has the longest continuous history of any area of the earth.

To the west it is bordered by the Mediterranean. South lies desert and then Egypt, once 'the granary of the world', and to the north-east, the cradle of the great empires of the ancient world. Astride the trade and military routes from Egypt to the north and north-east, Palestine's fortunes were inextricably bound up with those of the surrounding nations. For centuries she was a pawn and a prize as the balance of power shifted from one empire to its successor. Her greatness is that, in this situation, her people retained their identity as Israelites and survived as a religious entity.

A fertile plain extends inland from the Mediterranean for about fifteen miles. Barley, oats and wheat are cultivated and fruit trees: the fig, olive and grape vine have always been most highly valued. To the east, the foothills of the central mountain range rise out of the plain; these also are cultivated, and on the higher ground graze sheep and goats. Beyond the bleak mountains the land falls sharply away to the Jordan valley lying 700 feet below sea-level at Lake Galilee and 1,300 feet below at the Dead Sea. Further east again, on the far side of the Jordan, the land rises steeply, reaching a height of 4,000 feet in the neighbourhood of the Dead Sea. Because of high temperatures and the narrowness of the low-lying valley sudden, violent storms are frequent and make the main occupation of the area, fishing on Lake Galilee, at times a hazardous one.

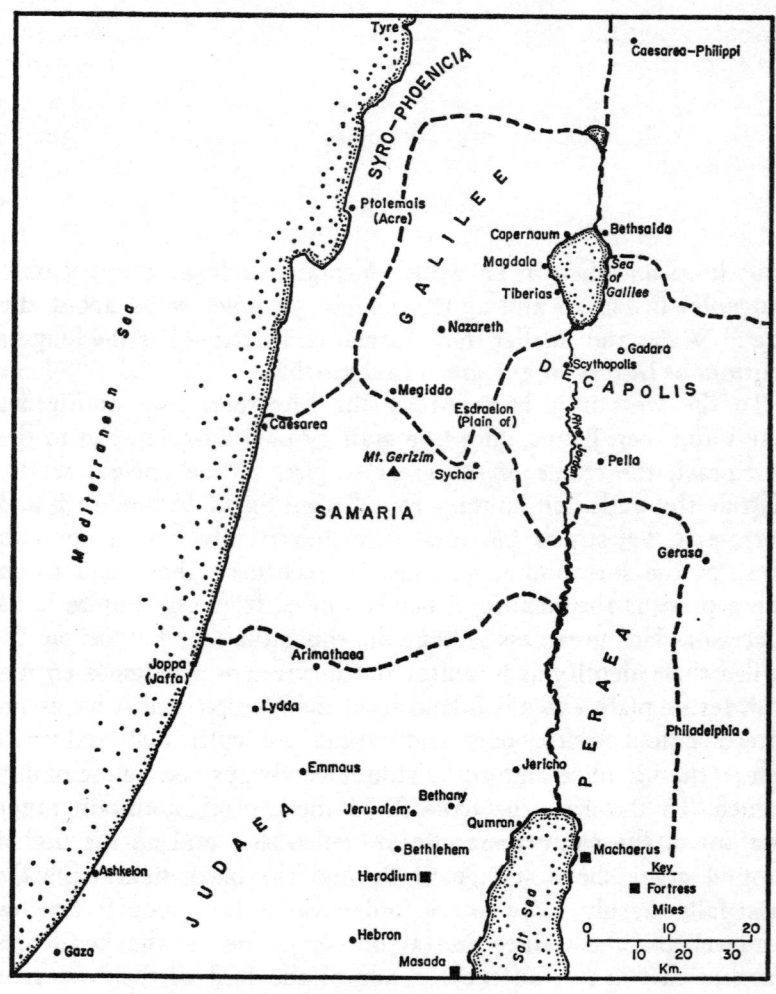

Map of Palestine

Of the places mentioned in the synoptic gospels, Bethlehem, Jericho, Jerusalem, and the nearby Mount of Olives, Bethany and Emmaus are in Judea, in the south and to the west of the Jordan and Dead Sea. Samaria lay immediately to the north of Judea; on its western shore was Caesarea where the Roman governors normally resided. North of Samaria is Galilee, with the towns or villages of Nazareth, Capernaum, Chorazin, Nain and Magdala (home of Mary Magdalene). Slightly north-east of Galilee lay Iturea, with Bethsaida near the head of the lake and Caesarea Philippi, built by the tetrarch Philip and named in honour of the Emperor, further north. North again is Mount Hermon, the possible site of the transfiguration, though Mount Tabor in Galilee has also been suggested as the 'high mountain' of Mark 9.2. East of Jordan was the predominantly Greek area of the Decapolis, and the Jewish Perea where John the Baptist met his death in the fortress at Machaerus. Idumea, mentioned in Mark 3.8 and home of the Edomites, lay to the south and Tyre and Sidon were on the coast of Phoenicia to the north-west of Galilee.

2. Chronology

The ancient world had no accurate method of reckoning dates nor our modern concern for a precise chronology.

Luke dated the beginning of Jesus' ministry in Galilee by 'the fifteenth year of Tiberius Caesar', but we are unable to fix this more precisely than between the years AD 26 and 28. By sifting all references in the gospels to the passage of time, scholars have concluded that Jesus' ministry lasted not less than two years and not more than slightly over three. His death therefore occurred between AD 28 and AD 31. The most probable date is in the spring of AD 30.

In the sixth century, the birth year of Jesus was taken as the base year for a new calendar of the Christian era. All other events in history would be dated from the year in which the Lord was born (AD = anno Domini, in the year of the Lord). This year was unfortunately not calculated correctly, and we have now the odd fact that Jesus was born before the year 4 BC (BC = before Christ)! We know that he was born in the reign of Herod the Great

3

(37-4 BC); Matthew 2.16 would suggest that it was at least two years before Herod's death. (See the fuller discussion on this question on pp. 141f.) Luke says that Jesus was about thirty years of age when he began his public ministry (3.23).

3. Historical and Political Situation

In 586 BC the Babylonians had captured and destroyed Jerusalem and deported many of the inhabitants of the kingdom of Judah (as it was then called; Judea corresponds roughly in area). Among them was the last king of the dynasty founded 400 years earlier by the great King David. But Jewish nationalism never died, and those born of Israelite parents continued to look for another David who would re-establish the kingdom.

Some of the descendants of the exiles returned from Babylon, and by 515 BC the temple had been rebuilt, though on a smaller and less magnificent scale than the first temple of King Solomon, and the city of Jerusalem made habitable. But the nation was never again to enjoy both independence and freedom from war. Persians, Greeks, Egyptians, Syrians, and, finally in 63 BC, Romans, were in turn her overlords except for a period of eighty war-torn years when she was ruled by her own Hasmonean priest-kings. In the absence of a king, the high priests gradually took secular as well as religious authority, and religion and nationalism continued to be inextricably related.

It was part of Rome's genius that she delegated authority to local rulers or administrative bodies. The Jewish high priest and a Council of Seventy (the Sanhedrin) were allowed to administer their holy city and temple. They jealously guarded this privilege, and opposed any display of nationalism or religious zeal which could be interpreted by Rome as a threat to the security of the State. In accordance with this same policy of decentralization Rome allowed, in AD 37, an Edomite, Herod, to make himself king in Palestine. He is known as Herod the Great but his people hated him, first because he was not a Jew but also for his extreme cruelty and because his rule was no lighter than direct rule from Rome. He tried to buy their favour by rebuilding the temple, twice the size of the post-exilic temple and of a truly remarkable grandeur so that the rabbis said that he who had not seen it had 'not seen a handsome building in his life'. It was begun in 20 BC, and finished only five years before its destruction by Rome in AD 70. Indirectly the Jews paid heavily for their temple, in taxation. The burden of a double taxation, paid to Rome and to the Herods, was to be one of the contributory factors in the revolt of AD 66 and the beginning of the four years' Jewish-Roman war which ended in the siege of Jerusalem, its complete destruction, and the end of the Jewish nation.

It was towards the end of the reign of the founder of the Herod dynasty that Jesus was born in Bethlehem of Judea, a village associated with King David.

Herod's three sons inherited his kingdom, though Rome would allow none of them the title of king. Archelaus became ethnarch of Judea, Samaria and Idumea; Antipas, tetrarch of Galilee and Perea; and Philip, tetrarch of the remaining territories in the north. In AD 6 Archelaus was deposed and a Roman procurator appointed to govern Judea. In AD 26 Pontius Pilate became the fifth procurator or governor. His appointment was terminated in AD 36 after a cruel massacre of Samaritans, though there had been earlier evidence of his unfitness for the position.

4. Worship in First-Century Judaism

The temple

The Israelites worshipped the God who had revealed himself to Moses as Yahweh (I am who I am – Ex.3). Their main worship was the offering of sacrificial animals in the temple in Jerusalem. The daily offerings, at 9 a.m. and 3 p.m. were on behalf of the whole community of Israel, whether living in Palestine or in other parts of the world, the 'Jews of the Dispersion', as these were called.

The three great annual festivals of Judaism, Passover, Weeks (Pentecost), and Tabernacles (Booths), brought to Jerusalem and the temple all Jews who were within travelling distance. The city of David, and the magnificence of Yahweh's temple on the holy Mount Sion of their forefathers, rekindled their national and religious hopes. The Feast of the Passover, in particular, reminded

5

them of how God had cared for Israel in the past; how long before he would once more act to deliver them?

As the indispensable officiants in the temple, the priests had become a powerful social as well as religious group long before the first century. The high priest was chosen from among them, though by long tradition from an exclusive group of 'high priestly families'. Some were members of the Sanhedrin, the only Jewish organization which had any real authority under Roman rule. They tended to be a conservative group – conservative of the religious traditions surrounding the temple and, many of them, conservative politically, satisfied unlike most Jews of the time with the Roman administration as long as it permitted the age-old ritual of the temple to continue.

The synagogue

During and after the exile in Babylon the synagogue was increasingly used as a sabbath meeting place for prayer and the study of the Hebrew scriptures. In synagogue schools children could learn Hebrew, which was no longer in common use, and the content and interpretation of the Mosaic Law. This included the commandments laid down by Moses and the vast accumulation since his day of 'traditions of the elders' which were equally binding to strict Jews.

The synagogues were administered by a body of elders, of whom one was the 'ruler' of the synagogue; there were no resident priests or rabbis. The ruler chose who would read from the treasured scrolls of the law and the prophets. The readings were followed by a paraphrase in Aramaic, called the *targum*, for the benefit of the majority who no longer understood Hebrew.

The synagogues had been instrumental in increasing devotion to Yahweh, and they had strengthened reverence for the scriptures, especially for the first five books, the *Torah* or law. These were believed to have been written by Moses. Although they were not, they did embody the law which he had given Israel and the subsequent additions and modifications necessary to adapt it to the Israelite's life in the promised land, Canaan or, as it was later called, Palestine.

The noble quality of life which attracted many non-Jews to Judaism was largely the fruit of synagogue worship and teaching.

The pattern of psalm, scripture and sermon, and prayers later provided the framework of Christian worship. The picture which the New Testament gives of a rigid rule-keeping was not typical of the best of Judaism.

5. Social and Religious Situation

In the first century Aramaic was the language commonly spoken in Palestine, though most people could understand Greek, the language of commerce and the market-place, especially in Galilee where there were many Greek-speaking Gentiles. Jesus taught in Aramaic, his mother-tongue. He was probably able to speak Greek when necessary, and would have had some knowledge of Hebrew. Latin was the official language of the Roman Empire, but few Jews would have known any more than the few words which had passed into common use, like praetorium, centurion, legion, denarius.

In the second century BC the Syrian king Antiochus III had begun to introduce the Greek language and culture into Palestine. This 'hellenization' was welcomed by some Jews as the door to the wider world, and feared by others as likely to alienate them from their own past. Those families from whom the high priest was chosen and the wealthy aristocracy favoured hellenization. In Jesus' day this group, the Sadducees, were small numerically but powerful socially. They were well represented on the Sanhedrin which, by its conduct of the temple, influenced the practice of religion; they were not, however, themselves sincerely religious.

A larger group, opposed to the Sadducees' religious ideas, political collaboration with Rome, and encouragement of the process of hellenization, was known in Jesus' day as the Pharisees. Originally they had been called 'the separated ones' because they separated themselves from all foreign and worldly influences and concentrated on the perfect performance of the law and traditions of the elders to counteract the anti-religious attitude of the Sadducees. The Pharisees honestly believed that their meticulous observance would one day bring about God's intervention to save his people.

Closely associated with the Pharisees were the teachers of the law. Most frequently referred to as 'scribes' in the gospels (but also as 'the doctors of the law', 'lawyers' or, simply 'rabbi' = teacher),

7

they were the professional interpreters, teachers and preservers of the religious past. They were greatly respected by the common people, whom they themselves despised as 'ignorant of the law'. As interpreters, it was they who laid down which activities infringed the sabbath rule of 'no work'. One of their rulings was that a woman might not look in a mirror on the sabbath because she might see a grey hair and be tempted to pull it out, and that would involve 'working'. As preservers of Israel's religious traditions, it was their responsibility to see that the next generation of teachers knew by heart the 613 commandments of the law. The tradition was preserved in the memories of men.

The fourth prominent group in the synoptic gospels, the Zealots, were like the Pharisees and scribes in that they were conservative of the traditions of Israel, though they were more interested in the national rather than the purely religious past. They were like the Sadducees in that they were involved in politics, though they were on the opposite side. The Sadducees supported the *status quo* because they derived their own prestige and authority from Rome's authority. The Zealots, on the other hand, were revolutionary nationalists waiting only for a leader before they rose against Rome to drive out all foreign influence and restore the kingdom to Israel.

The first century AD, like the twentieth century, had its own economic, political, social and religious tensions and the gospels must be studied against that background.

We need also to understand something of the 'world-view' of the people of that time. They looked at the world about them with very different presuppositions from those of our scientific space-age. For instance, they thought of the universe as occupying three 'storeys' in space. The gods inhabited the upper storey, and the region below the earth was the abode of the dead and of spirits harmful to men. The first Christians, however, spoke of God as present everywhere and as dwelling in men's hearts, and when they used the imagery of ascension in speaking of Jesus' presence with the Father after his resurrection, we need not necessarily infer that they thought of a literal raising into the sky. 'Ascended into heaven' was the natural way of speaking of spiritual closeness to God.

The first century did not have our knowledge of cause and effect. Any behaviour that was not normal to human beings they explained as spirit-possession. It was also believed that only some serious secret sin could have brought the sufferer to such a plight. There are frequent references to Jesus healing the sick and restoring disturbed minds by getting rid of an evil spirit. The diagnosis would be different today with our knowledge of the effect of bacteria and its own glandular secretions on the human body; but whatever the method of diagnosis it is the healing that is important. Jesus' power to forgive sins, calm the disturbed minds of the mentally ill, and restore diseased bodies to health was due, so his contemporaries believed, to God, the ultimate source of all power. These healings were not looked on as wonders, but as signs that God's kingdom of love was made present in the world through his life of self-giving.

Another feature of the gospels which can be understood only in the context of first-century Judaism is the apocalyptic imagery associated with judgment. Since evil was the work of unclean spirits, seeds sown in men's hearts by the devil, at the end of the age God would send his *angelos*, messengers, to act as reapers, separating out the worthless weeds that were fit only for burning from those whose lives had eternal value. Our attempts to account for the existence of sin and suffering have reached a different conclusion, but the problem is still as acute for us and our solutions no more adequate.

The Jews, and consequently the first Christians, had faith that God would be ultimately victorious over evil and suffering, and that goodness and righteousness would be vindicated on the day of judgment which would end the present age of earthly existence.

REVISION QUESTIONS

1. List the four main religious, social or political groups in first-century Palestine, and describe their chief characteristics.

2. How did the worship of the temple in Jerusalem differ from that of the synagogues of the villages and towns?

3. Briefly describe how Jerusalem and the various districts of Palestine were governed in the time of Jesus.

4. In what ways do first-century beliefs about the universe, the problem of good and evil, and the existence of suffering differ from ours?

2 The 'Good News' and the Three Synoptic Gospels

1. Expectation

One of the characteristics of the Hebrews was their expectation that God would act decisively in the world to save them by bringing about his kingdom on earth. They had various ideas on the way in which this 'Day of the Lord' would come, and the prophets had warned that it would not be a day of rejoicing only but also of judgment since they would then know how far short they had fallen of the covenant ideal of mercy, justice and brotherly love. Closely associated with this expectation of the kingdom was the belief in the coming of a Saviour who would possess the Spirit of God.

In early times in Israel, a man was anointed with oil as a sign that God had chosen him for some special purpose, such as king, or prophet. The expected deliverer was sometimes spoken of as 'messiah', that is, 'anointed one'. The Greek word which translated this idea was *christos*, from which we get the English word Christ.

The prophet Isaiah had spoken of the one who was to come as a servant, God's servant, who would willingly accept suffering as the means of saving his people. Isaiah had described what he would do for other men as 'the good tidings' (Isa. 61.1-2).

2. The Proclamation of the Good Tidings

Jesus the carpenter of Nazareth began his public preaching by announcing 'the time is fulfilled, and the kingdom of God is at hand'. In the synagogue he read Isaiah's prophecy and then said to the people: 'Today this scripture has been fulfilled in your hearing' (Luke 4.16-30). This was an extraordinary claim for a Jew to make. It was as if he was saying that the Spirit of the Lord would enable *him* to fulfil the age-old expectation.

Isaiah 61.1-2 and Luke 4.18-19 both state that the good tidings or news would go to the poor, the blind, the captive and the oppressed. When we study the life of Jesus of Nazareth we see that he interpreted this metaphorically as well as literally: the 'poor' were the outcast and those in need of any kind; the 'blind', all in need of spiritual perception or insight; the 'captives', those bound by their own weakness or sin. He saw the task before him as that of bringing freedom from all that oppressed or diminished human existence.

His first followers experienced this freedom. They wanted to share it with others. They began to proclaim the good news that God was at work amongst his people in and through this man Jesus. It was natural that they should use Isaiah's word 'good tidings': *euangelion* in Greek. When the *euangelion* in time reached England it was brought by 'evangelists', those who told the good news. The Old English word *godspel* was used to translate it, and from this comes our word 'gospel'. The Christian gospel is the good news that the day of the Lord has indeed come, and that men can receive power to help them live their lives as they are meant to be lived, by sharing in the life of the Christ.

3. The Oral Tradition

At first the gospel was passed on by word of mouth. In the first century few men and women had opportunity to obtain or read books. They were expensive and laborious to make: the paper had first to be made from split reeds laid one across the other at right angles and pressed together, and then the 'book' had to be written by hand. The consequence was that memories became retentive and accurate because there was only the spoken word from which to learn,[1] and everyone had plenty of practice in memorizing.

[1] 'The rabbis had a saying that the ideal pupil was like a limed (that is, a concrete) cistern, which never loses a drop of water that is put into it. The obligation of the pupil to reproduce to the next generation exactly what his

The spoken gospel spread rapidly through Palestine, where Jesus the Christ had lived and taught, in the years following his death. If any evangelist made mistakes in reporting what the Master had said, there would almost certainly be someone in the audience who had heard him in person and could challenge the mis-reporting. The period in which the gospel was thus passed on is called the period of the oral tradition.

With much telling and re-telling, his teaching and the stories about him began to take on a fixed form, and unimportant details like the time and place where a particular incident occurred, and the names of those involved in it, were dropped out. Such details were not essential to the 'good news' which was for all men, of all times and places.

Inevitably, each evangelist would tend to repeat most frequently his own favourite memories of Jesus. He would also select from the oral tradition the particular story or incident or saying which would best convey to his audience of the moment the importance for them of the Christian gospel. Thus, as time wore on, the oral tradition would vary slightly from place to place.

4. The First Written Records

The time came when it was desirable to have this information written down.

Perhaps the first written document was the passion narrative. The account of the betrayal, trial, crucifixion and resurrection of Jesus had been repeated by his followers when they met together to worship God in the way that he had taught them. It was therefore easy to write it down just as it was recited in worship. We can see traces of 'liturgical language', that is, the balanced and rhythmic language necessary for speaking aloud in worship, in the passion narratives of the gospels.

Then, as the teaching and missionary needs of the church required, collections were made of Jesus' teaching on various subjects. For example, pagans who became interested in the Christian

master had taught him extended not only to ideas but even to the manner of expression and the choice of words.' Bruce Metzger, *The New Testament*, Lutterworth Press 1965, p.50.

gospel would want to know how he had forgiven those who came to him, wanting to begin life afresh. Those being prepared for admission into the Christian fellowship by baptism would need to know what the Lord had taught about prayer and relationship with the Father.

Collections of stories of his healings were also important for teaching purposes, as Jesus taught not only in word, but also by deed.

As the gospel spread outside Palestine and attracted Gentiles (that is, those who were not Jews), they naturally wanted to know what the Lord had done for people like themselves. As opposition to the new teaching grew inside Palestine, it was necessary to be able to show exactly what Jesus had said on the subject of the Jewish law: that he had not set out to destroy, but to fulfil, its original purpose.

A collection of texts from the Hebrew scriptures which seemed to be fulfilled by some detail of Jesus' life was also made. These 'proof-texts' were regarded by his followers as evidence that he was the messiah, since his deeds or words fulfilled the old prophecies. We cannot always see the relevance of the proof-texts, or regard them as evidence, but Matthew made extensive use of them in his Gospel. He was writing for Palestinians who were unwilling to accept that an obscure carpenter, who had been crucified as a common criminal, could be the long-awaited messiah, and he needed the evidence of their own scriptures to support his claim about Jesus.

Thus the first written records were made for the purposes of worship, teaching, explanation, and defence of the Christian gospel. They were not particularly concerned with biographical details, nor were they in any chronological order.

5. The Gospels

About a generation after Jesus' death it was thought advisable to collate all the oral and written material into a connected and comprehensive 'book'.

Eye-witnesses were beginning to die, and it was realized that a large-scale persecution of well-known Christians could wipe out the evangelists. Furthermore, the new teaching was now widespread throughout the Roman Empire and a standard and authoritative account of the gospel was needed.

The form of the material available determined the sort of book which could be written. It could not be biography, since only the last two or three years of his life were known. It could not be history, since dates and places and the names of people he met with during his mission had not been preserved. It had to be, in fact, an entirely new sort of literature, just as it recorded an entirely new sort of event in the history of the world. It was – gospel.

Mark began his book with the words: 'The beginning of the *euangelion* of Jesus Christ ...' In time it came to be called 'The Gospel according to Mark', that is, Mark's version of the good tidings that God 'has visited and redeemed his people'.

Other versions of the gospel were written, perhaps because the already existing books were not known in a particular locality, and to meet the different needs of other groups, or areas, to which the Christian good news had spread. Four came to be generally accepted: the Gospel according to Matthew, the Gospel according to Mark, the Gospel according to Luke, and the Gospel according to John.

REVISION QUESTIONS

1. Write brief notes on the words Christ, gospel, evangelist.
2. What do you know of the period of oral tradition of the Christian gospel?
3. What were some of the causes of the political and economic unrest in Palestine under Roman domination?

3 *The Synoptic Gospels and their Relationship*

The first three gospels, Matthew, Mark and Luke, have much in common with one another. They describe Jesus' ministry from much the same point of view, and contain similar information, which is for the most part recorded in the same order, and sometimes even in the same words. Because of these similarities they have been given the name 'synoptic', which is derived from the Greek prefix *sun-*, meaning together or alike, and the Greek word *opsis*, seeing. Matthew, Mark and Luke can be printed in parallel columns (and thus 'seen together') and their similarities and differences studied.

The fourth, the Gospel according to John, is different in many ways and makes its own quite distinctive contribution to our understanding of the 'one gospel of Jesus Christ'. In this book we shall consider only the information given in the Gospels according to Matthew, Mark and Luke.

1. The Synoptic Problem

What is the relationship of the synoptic gospels? How are we to account for their similarities and their differences, for they were sufficiently unlike for the church to want to preserve all three.

If you look at the page index of the Bible you will see that the Gospel of Mark is about two-thirds the length of either of the other two. Did he abbreviate the 'good news'? Did the others have access to information unknown to Mark? Or did the needs of the churches for which they wrote oblige them to include more than Mark had thought necessary for the people for whom he wrote?

When these three gospels are printed in parallel columns so that one can compare them and consider the possible reasons for the omissions, additions and alterations, it is possible to begin to form an opinion about these questions. A book which prints the similar passages side by side is called a *synopsis*.[1] Another useful aid is *A Diagram of Synoptic Relationships*,[2] in which the three gospels are represented verse by verse in blocks of different colour according to whether they appear in all three, or in two, or in one only. If a verse occurs in only one, the colour by which it is represented indicates if it is in Matthew, or Mark, or Luke. When a verse is in more than one gospel connecting lines enable one to see whether it is in the same order.

The first striking point one notices is that almost the whole of Mark is found in either Matthew or Luke. In fact, about 95% of Mark is found in Matthew and 60% in Luke. On the whole the common material is in the same sequence, though there are exceptions to this. Sometimes we find minor alterations to Mark's language: abbreviations or expansions which may have been an attempt to make the meaning clearer or, perhaps, to improve Mark's rather colloquial Greek.

What conclusions are we to draw? Did Mark take from Matthew and Luke just what he considered important? But, in that case, we should have to say that he did not think Matthew's three chapters of Jesus' teaching in the sermon on the mount important since they are not found in the Gospel of Mark. Alternatively, are we to conclude that Matthew and Luke used Mark's book as their main source of information, and inserted into it what was necessary for their own purposes?

These questions raise the further one: which gospel was written first? Tradition says that the Gospel according to Matthew was the earliest, and of course it is placed first in order in the New Testament. On the other hand, the majority of scholars today think that Mark was written first, in Rome in approximately AD 65, and that Matthew and Luke thought they could not do better than use it as a framework for their longer works. Into this basic source they incorporated such other information about Jesus' teachings, healings and other activities as would best enable them to make the

[1] A clear synopsis is *Gospel Parallels*, published by Nelson. It uses the Revised Standard Version of the Bible.
[2] Allan Barr, A *Diagram of Synoptic Relationships*, published by T. & T. Clark.

16

gospel intelligible and acceptable to those for whom they wrote. You should try to form your own opinion on the evidence of the gospels themselves, though this would be easier to do if you could read them in the original Greek in which they were written. Although Jesus spoke Aramaic, the language of Palestine, the gospel was translated into Greek before any of our present gospels were written; Greek was the tongue more universally understood in the Roman Empire and it was necessary if his message was to reach the Gentile world.

2. The Gospel according to Mark

One-third of Mark's book consists of the passion narrative, that is, the story of the last week of Jesus' life on earth. One could almost say that his death and resurrection was itself the 'good news', since it was proof that a man could live a life of such quality that it was victorious over the worst that evil could do, and over man's final enemy, death; and, if one man, why not, with God's help, all men? It is as though Mark added his first thirteen chapters to explain the circumstances that brought about the death of such a man, and to show the quality of his life which God had 'vindicated' by raising him from the dead.

The word 'passion', in the sense in which it is used of Jesus Christ's suffering and death, comes from the Latin word for suffering. The first Christians believed that Christ's sufferings which were caused by human sin and evil had power to heal that sin and take away the destructive power of evil. This is partly the reason why they recalled his passion, by reciting over the details of his betrayal, trial, death and resurrection, Sunday by Sunday when they met to commemorate his resurrection on 'the first day of the week'. When anything is repeated often enough, especially aloud and in public, it tends to take on a fixed, stylized form. When this happens to the language of worship we have what is called liturgical language. Mark would not have to look far to find the source for the last one-third of his record of what God had done for man through Jesus.

For the rest, Mark could draw on the oral traditions of the area in which he lived, and on any of the written collections known to him. Reports of near-contemporary writers say that he also obtained information from the apostle Peter, who is believed to have been killed in Rome about AD 64. Probably it was the danger to men like Peter during the reign of Emperor Nero that made Mark's work an urgent necessity: their memories must be preserved for future generations. Taking into consideration all the evidence available, it seems most satisfactory to give to the Gospel according to Mark the approximate date of AD 65.

Of course, we do not really know who Mark was. Some early writers suggested that he was the John Mark who accompanied Paul on one of his journeys and who is mentioned in the Acts of the Apostles and possibly in some of Paul's letters. It is unlikely that a gospel would have been attributed to a relatively unknown Christian unless he were in fact the author, though we cannot be absolutely certain about the author of any of the gospels because the earliest manuscripts did not always bear the author's name. However, whoever Mark was, he wrote because he was convinced that the power of God was at work in the Jesus of Nazareth who called himself 'Son of man', and whom later Christians called 'Son of God'.

3. The Four-Document Hypothesis

A second fact which emerges from a comparison of the synoptic gospels is that Matthew and Luke seem to have used a further common source, in addition to Mark, which probably consisted of *logia*, or sayings, of Jesus. We have no copy of such a document, but the similarities in Matthew and Luke have led scholars to infer its existence. It is sometimes referred to as 'Q', from the German *quelle*, source. Since there is no proof that 'Q' ever did exist as a written document, it is a hypothesis to account for the relationship between Matthew and Luke.

There are further stories, incidents, and teaching than can be accounted for by Mark and 'Q'. The symbol 'M' has been given to the information which Matthew alone has, and 'L' to that exclusive to Luke.

The four-document hypothesis is an attempt to explain the synoptic problem (see pp. 15-17). A hypothesis is a theory to

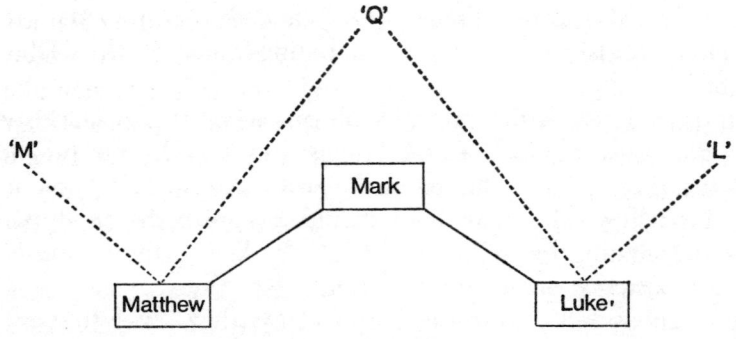

Diagram showing the sources of the
synoptic gospels

account for the known facts. Scientists prefer the hypothesis which
is the simplest one able to account for all the evidence. For many
scholars today the four-document hypothesis provides the most
acceptable theory of the origins and relationships of the synoptic
gospels; but of course it must remain a hypothesis while our only
knowledge of 'Q', 'M', and 'L' is deduced from the gospels themselves.

4. The Gospel according to Matthew

Matthew quotes frequently from the Hebrew scriptures and is fond
of adding to a healing or saying of Jesus such a statement as: '... as
it is written in the prophet ...', or '... this was to fulfil the
prophecy ...'[3]

He collected Jesus' teaching and comments on the Jewish law
into three chapters (5-7), and presented it as if it had been given
as one long sermon on a mountain. In this sermon on the mount,
as it is called, Jesus is shown as the re-interpreter and fulfiller of
the law which God had given Moses at Mount Sinai: 'Think not
that I have come to abolish the law and the prophets; I have not
come to abolish them but to fulfil them' (Matt. 5.17). Jesus is the
'prophet greater than Moses' of Hebrew expectation (Deut. 18.15-
18).

It is emphasized in this gospel that Jesus of Nazareth is the
Christ,[4] God's answer to Israel's ancient religious hope. He is also

[3] Examples may be found in Matt. 8.17; 13.35; 15.7; 21.4; 21.16.
[4] As, for example, by the repetition in Matt. 1.1,16,17,18.

'son of David, son of Abraham' (1.1), and thus heir to the great hero-king of Israel, and to the founding-father of the Hebrew nation.

In these ways Matthew conveys his conviction that the Christian Lord and Master is the messiah promised by the Hebrew prophets and the three greatest figures in Hebrew history. His purpose is that his fellow-Palestinian Jews should recognize the anointed of God and, finding in his life and death the key to the meaning of human existence, enter into 'salvation'.

We can see reflected in the Gospel of Matthew the bitterness of the first Christians who thought of themselves as true Jews because they followed the messiah, and yet were rejected by their own religious leaders. Those who could not accept him as messiah regarded Jesus as a dangerous teacher; one of the accusations at his trial was that he had been 'perverting the nation' (Luke 23.2). In AD 85 his followers were banned from the synagogues. Because of his bitterness, it is likely Matthew was writing around the year AD 85.

Tradition says that Matthew was Levi the tax collector who became a disciple of Jesus. But would a disciple and eye-witness use Mark's book as his main source? Even the 'M' material does not suggest an eye-witness. Furthermore, would Levi the tax collector have had the necessary knowledge of the Jewish law to set out so systematically the teaching in the sermon on the mount? Matthew the apostle is believed to have written down many sayings of Jesus in Aramaic. It is possible that this *logia*-document, translated into Greek, was incorporated into the gospel and gave the name of Matthew to the whole.

5. The Gospel according to Luke

What was Luke's purpose in writing his gospel? Jesus had presupposed in his hearers a knowledge of the religious, social and moral customs of Palestine and familiarity with the Hebrew scriptures. As time went on and the Christian gospel was proclaimed to Greeks, Romans and other Gentiles, a re-statement of it was necessary. For example, the word Christ did not have for them the significance messiah had for Jews; the idea behind the word had to be made clear in some other way.

But first they had to be assured that it was relevant to them. Luke's first aim was to commend the gospel to the educated Gentile world as something they need not be ashamed of accepting, and as God's offer to them no less than to the Jews.

He began in the conventional style of the current Greek literature (1.1-4). He dated the events he was about to narrate with references to well-known secular facts: the Roman Emperor's accession year, and the name of the governor in office in the province of Syria, of which Galilee and Judea were part (3.1). His dedication to 'most excellent Theophilus' may be a commendation to an important official (though as the word means literally 'lover of God' it could be a pseudonym for any Gentile seeking God).

Jesus is presented as saviour of all mankind, and as the Spirit-filled Son of God who would give to others the same Spirit in whose power he had lived. He is descended not only from the human families of Abraham and David, but from '... the son of Adam, the son of God' (3.18); that is, from the origins of the human race. In ancient mythology Adam (the root is the Hebrew word for man) stood for the first of *homo sapiens*. Luke wants his readers to know that the Christ was not merely a Jewish teacher; his words are of significance for all men because there is divine authority in all he said and did.

We do not know for certain who Luke was, or when he wrote. It is quite likely that he was Paul's friend and doctor Lucius, and that he wrote about AD 75. He is also the author of the Acts of the Apostles.[5]

REVISION QUESTIONS

1. What is the 'four-document hypothesis'?

2. Write an essay on the sources available to the writers of the synoptic gospels.

3. What do you know about the authorship and dating of the synoptic gospels?

4. What was the particular purpose Matthew had in mind when he wrote his gospel? What was Luke's aim in writing his version of the one Christian gospel?

[5] Compare Acts 1.1 with Luke 1.1-4.

4 *The Man who was 'Good News'*

Having seen something of how the gospels came into being, we must now ask who was this man whose life was, so his contemporaries thought, good news for all other men.

The gospel only began to be proclaimed when a man who had been publicly crucified and buried was recognized as having been raised to life by God. As his friends looked back over what they knew of his life, they realized that this man had been different from other men always in the quality of his concern for others and in his dependence on God. It is easy to be wise after the event. They now saw that there had been certain pointers which, in the light of the resurrection, took on new significance. It was God's action in raising Jesus of Nazareth to life which *was* the good news.

How can we put ourselves in a similar position to those men of AD 30, so that we can study the events of Jesus' ministry in the light of the final event which had been for them the beginning – the resurrection? A sensible way of using this book would be to begin at the end, with the chapters on the crucifixion and resurrection, and only then to study the chapters on Jesus' life and teaching. But, instead, let us look briefly at some of those significant pointers before we begin our detailed study of the synoptic gospels so that we understand something of the conviction that gave them birth – that God had intervened in human history through the life of the carpenter of Nazareth.

The baptism of Jesus (Mark 1.11) At his baptism by John the Baptist, something happened which convinced Jesus that his relationship with God, and consequently his mission in life, was a special one. He believed that the Spirit of God came to him, and he understood that God was saying 'Thou art my beloved Son; with thee I am well pleased.'

His teaching about the kingdom of God (Mark 1.15)   He then began to proclaim that the time had come for the kingdom of God to be established. This was no political rallying-call (although Israel's national and religious hopes had always been closely allied) for the word used, in Greek *basileia,* is an abstract noun and was not used of a territorial kingdom. The kingdom which Jesus proclaimed was the decisive action of God in the world, but it could be effective only as men accepted the reign of God in their hearts and allowed it to transform their lives. Sometimes he spoke as if it were already present, and his 'mighty works' evidence of its power at work through him; at other times as if it would not be wholly established until all men accepted 'thy will be done' as the guiding principle of their lives. This was to be his mission in life.

The call of the disciples (Mark 1.17)   Jesus needed the help of men who were prepared to give up their own way of life and share his. That they could so readily abandon their ordinary means of earning a living to share the life of a wandering teacher is some indication of his compelling attraction for them.

'You are the Christ' (Mark 8.29)   One of these men, Peter, was the first to begin to see that their new friend and master was doing all that had been expected of the messiah: he forgave sins, gave sight to the blind, enabled the lame to walk, healed men believed to be possessed of destructive spirits, befriended the friendless outcasts of society. Surely he was the Christ.

Transfiguration (Mark 9.2-8)   Shortly after this new understanding of Peter's, he and James and John Zebedee had a vision of Jesus talking to Moses and Elijah and they suddenly realized that he was the fulfilment of all the law and the prophets had been trying to teach. At first Peter thought this was the end of the road: they could stop there in the moment of worship and vision; but from the overshadowing cloud they seemed to hear, 'This is my beloved Son; listen to him.' Moses and Elijah faded from the vision and they saw Jesus only. There was to be a new beginning, following the life and words of the beloved Son. What Jesus had understood at his baptism was now understood by others.

The Son of man (Mark 10.45) He, however, described himself as 'the Son of man' who had come to serve and save men. This term had been used in the Book of Daniel in the Hebrew scriptures of the true people of God who stood before him in judgment, but also in glory. It seemed to be connected in Jesus' mind with the necessity for his suffering and death, by which human evil would stand judged. When his life of self-giving was vindicated by God, he would lead his people into 'glory' – the presence of God.

The night before he died (Mark 14.22-5) At supper with his closest friends, Jesus took the bread and blessed it in the customary way by offering it to God, and broke it and gave it to them with the strange words: 'Take; this is my body.' Then he blessed the wine and gave it, saying: 'This is my blood of the covenant, which is poured out for many.' The significance of what he had done at this last supper became clear the next day when his body was crucified and his blood shed in agony.

After the resurrection, his friends began to break bread together and share the cup of wine, and they found that he was still present with them. They could only ask in wonder: *who was it whose life lived on in them through this covenant meal?*

Life out of death (Mark 14.32-6) After the supper they went to the garden of Gethsemane where Jesus prayed that there might be some way of completing his mission other than by dying. But at the end of his prayer he was able to accept that his life was the seed which had to fall into the ground and apparently die so that new life for others might spring from it.

Was he the Christ, or a blasphemer? (Mark 14.61-4) This question is the challenge of the Christian gospel, and everyone has to make his own response to it. Jesus answered 'I am' when the high priest put the question 'Are you the Christ, the Son of the Blessed?' Those who heard him said he deserved to die. A Roman

24

centurion in charge of the execution party said, 'Truly this man was Son of God.' (Mark 15.39).

Resurrection (Mark 16.6-8) On the third day after his death women found his tomb empty. An unidentified man told them, 'Do not be amazed; you seek Jesus of Nazareth, who was crucified. He has risen, he is not here ...' They fled in fear and astonishment. Such awe as this began the spread of the gospel: *who could this be whom God had raised from the dead?*

Mark wrote his gospel after many years of meeting the risen Lord in the breaking of bread. He wanted to put on permanent record that the carpenter of Nazareth was not only the Christ, or the greatest son of mankind, but also the beloved Son of God. Whatever the centurion's words had meant at the moment he spoke them, to Mark they expressed all that he had come to believe: that death had been 'the beginning of the gospel of Jesus Christ, the Son of God' (Mark 1.1).

REVISION QUESTIONS

1. Find out all you can about the expressions 'Son of man' and 'Son of God'. Why did Jesus use the former of himself? Why did the early Christians come to call him 'Son of God'?

2. What did Jesus mean by the 'kingdom of God'? Why did he sometimes speak as if it were already present on earth, and at other times (as for instance in the Lord's Prayer) as if it were still in the future?

(The questions in 1. above would be useful in class discussion.)

5   *Jesus in Galilee: the Beginning of the Mission*

Mark 1.1-15 and parallel passages

With this chapter we begin the detailed study of the synoptic gospels. We shall follow Mark, but note any additional information which Matthew and Luke give so that we gain a comprehensive picture of Jesus Christ in the synoptic gospels. In part two of the book we shall deal with events and teaching which Mark does not mention at all. It is most important that the biblical references throughout the book be followed up.

In this chapter we shall study John the Baptist's preparatory work, and Jesus' own experiences immediately before his ministry in Galilee. For the sake of completeness, all the synoptic gospel information about John will be included in this chapter.

1. *The Preaching of John the Baptist*
Mark 1.2-8; Matt. 3.1-12; Luke 3.1-20

The first Christians understood John the Baptist's role in terms of the prophecies in Isaiah 40.3 and Malachi 4.5-6. Isaiah had said that before the glory of God could be revealed on earth and man's war against him end, a warning 'voice' would go through the land. Malachi thought that it would be Elijah's, calling men to repentance.

With his camel-hair cloak and leather girdle, John looked like Elijah.[1] Elijah had withstood King Ahab[2] and his cruel Queen Jezebel; John bravely denounced Herod for marrying his own brother's wife. He also preached repentance, telling men to turn themselves to God so that they could be forgiven. Jesus called John a second Elijah (Matt. 17.10-13).

[1] 2 Kings 1.8.   [2] 1 Kings 21.

26

As John went through the countryside preaching: 'Repent, for the kingdom of heaven is at hand', he had a dramatic effect on the people of Judea and its great city of Jerusalem (Mark 1.5). He used vivid metaphors to challenge his hearers to change what was wrong in their lives (Matt. 3.7,10,12). Popular opinion held that the day of judgment was only for the heathen, but John said there was no automatic protection in being 'a son of Abraham'; *every* tree that did not bear good fruit was cut down as worthless. Luke reports John's specific advice to those who asked what fruits of repentance they should show in their lives (Luke 3.10-14).

2. *Jesus Comes to John to be Baptized*
Mark 1.9-11; Matt. 3.13-17; Luke 3.21-2

The Jews baptized any non-Jews who wished to practise the Jewish religion and mix on equal social terms with them. This baptism was thought of as washing away their 'Gentile uncleanness'. They also practised a ritual washing when they themselves had been defiled by contact with Gentiles or unclean animals. But John's baptism was quite unlike either of these customs. It was for Jews whether or not they were 'ritually unclean'; and it brought forgiveness to those who were truly repentant. ('Ritual' is the religious ceremony used in worship. It used to be thought that a man was unfit to come before his god if he had been in contact with certain taboo people or objects; to first-century Jews certain animals, and any object which might have been in contact with men and women of any other race, were 'taboo' or 'unclean'. Jesus later taught that nothing from outside a man could make him unclean in this religious sense, but only his own thoughts or actions.)

Why did Jesus come to John for baptism? Presumably, he wanted to show that he was in agreement with John's call to repentance, and that he identified himself with those who were turning to God as a result of it.

John had said that the one who would come after him would baptize with the Holy Spirit. Immediately after his baptism Jesus is shown receiving the Spirit. The pictorial language is full of symbolic meaning: 'the heavens opened' is a way of stating that it was God's gift that Jesus received; 'descending upon him' suggests that it came to him for ever, unlike the occasional coming of 'the Spirit of the Lord' in the Old Testament; 'like a dove', that the Spirit would work quietly and peacefully through his human nature, pervading all his actions and words, unlike, for example, its effect on Samson and Saul. The 'voice from heaven' is Jesus' call to do God's work: now he must leave the obscurity of the village carpenter's bench and accept the dangerous limelight of public preaching.

3. Temptation

Mark 1.12-13; Matt. 4.1-11; Luke 4.1-13

John has prepared the way, and Jesus has accepted his call. How is he to set about his work for God's people?

Although there was general expectation of the messiah, there were very different ideas about what he would be like. The first-century Zealots looked for another King David, who would lead them in a successful revolt against the hated Romans. Others thought of the messiah more as a phantasy or magic figure, who would solve their problems and remove their enemies without their having to do much to help themselves. Jesus had now to decide just how he was to deliver his people. We see him rejecting three temptingly easy, but ultimately inadequate, ways of fulfilling the task God had given him.

Mark's account is very brief but it paints a graphic picture of those days of inner struggle. It seemed to Jesus that he was fighting against the devil, or with wild beasts; and, when it was over, that God had supported him all the while. We still today sometimes say of a particularly strong temptation, 'the devil tempted me'. The word 'angel' comes from the Greek word *angelos*, messenger of God. 'Forty days' was an idiom for a long period of time.

The fuller accounts in Matthew and Luke portray Jesus resisting the temptation to capture popular support by:

(i) *bribery* (giving men prosperity and an easy life, symbolized by the temptation to turn the small, flat, white stones of the Judean hills into bread);

(ii) *force* (with the support of the Zealots he might have won an earthly kingdom in which he could have established political freedom and just economic conditions); and

28

(iii) *magic* (by throwing himself off the highest point of the Jerusalem temple without hurt he would have convinced many that he was messiah).

But he knew that a sudden, unearned plenty would not solve the real problems of human poverty. Nor could even good ends be achieved by force without doing evil (symbolized in the worship of the devil). Nor could men who followed him for the wrong motives be helped in their greatest need, which was to be able to trust God and co-operate with one another in changing all that was unjust in society; to have given way to the third temptation would have been to tempt God, not to trust him.

All three gospels emphasize that the Spirit was with Jesus as he wrestled with the question of how he was to live out his Sonship. Luke says not only that he was led by the Spirit into the lonely place where he faced the temptations, but that 'he returned in the power of the Spirit into Galilee, and a report concerning him went out through all the surrounding country' (Luke 4.1,14). Temptation had strengthened him; he had grown stronger through facing it.

4. *The Beginning of Jesus' Teaching in Galilee*
Mark 1.14-15; 6.1-6; Matt. 4.12-17; 13.54-8; Luke 4.14-30

John had baptized in Judea, near the Dead Sea in the south of Palestine, and Jesus must have fought out the temptations in the uninhabited area to the east of the River Jordan. When John was arrested by Herod Jesus returned to Galilee in the north and made Capernaum on the northern shore of the lake his headquarters. He had seen in John's arrest the signal that the time had come for him to begin his life's work. His message was similar to John's (cf. Matt. 3.2—4.17).

Many were astonished at the authority with which he spoke; but others took offence because, after all, he was only the carpenter's son, someone they had known all their lives. Luke has told of one such occasion in the synagogue at Nazareth.[3] It was a comforting thought that *one day* God would intervene in the affairs of men;

[3] Luke 4.16-30.

it was more difficult to accept that he wanted to do it *now*, in their own lives.

5. John's Imprisonment and Death

Mark 6.14-29; Matt. 14.1-12; 11.2-19; Luke 3.19-20; 7.18-35

Herod Antipas had become tetrarch of Galilee on the death of his father, Herod the Great, in the year 4 BC. When John criticized his callous behaviour in divorcing his legal wife to marry his half-brother's wife (she was also his niece), Herod had him thrown into prison. Herodias herself hated John and wanted him dead, but Herod feared to antagonize the people who respected John as a prophet. Herodias' opportunity for revenge came when Herod promised her daughter Salome anything she asked (Mark 6.21-29).

While in prison John had begun to worry that he might have been wrong. Was Jesus the one who was to come? Or had his whole life been wasted? (Matt. 11.2-19; Luke 7.18-35). He sent his friends to ask: 'Are you he who is to come, or shall we look for another?' Jesus let his actions speak for him: 'Go and tell John what you hear and see ...' He knew that John would recognize that Isaiah's prophecy of good tidings was being fulfilled, and that his preparatory work had not been in vain; the kingdom which John had announced was now a present fact for the blind who saw and the lame who walked and the lepers who were cleansed. Men could enter God's kingdom as sons by sharing in Jesus' Sonship.

REVISION QUESTIONS

1. What part did John the Baptist play at the beginning of Jesus' ministry?

2. Write an obituary notice for John, including all facts known about his adult life.

3. Describe the temptations as reported in the synoptic gospels. What ideas about the messiah was Jesus considering and rejecting?

4. Recount in detail what happened in the synagogue at Nazareth when Jesus read from the prophet Isaiah.

6 *Challenge and Response*

Mark 1.16—3.12 and parallel passages

Mark's first chapters show us the three types of response which Jesus' contemporaries made to the challenge he put before them.

A few men left their homes and jobs to become disciples, and learn from him what it meant to accept God's sovereignty in their lives.

Ordinary men and women recognized in his healing and forgiving, God's love reaching out to make them whole. Healing, wholeness, holiness (these words are derived from the one root) were, to them, signs of the presence of God's kingdom on earth.

However, Jesus' outspokenness and determination to help all in need, whatever their race, religion or social status, brought him into conflict with the religious and political 'conservatives'. The Sadducees were the political conservatives; they had no quarrel with Rome as long as they were permitted to administer the temple and city of Jerusalem. He was to earn their enmity during the last week of his life in Jerusalem, but they do not figure in the early years of his ministry in Galilee. The Pharisees were the religious conservatives; they had erected their own interpretation of the law of Moses into a religion and they felt threatened by Jesus' more demanding religion of love: of a personal response of love towards God and men. The scribes, the official teachers of Judaism, shared the Pharisees' objection. Their hatred grew as the people's respect for Jesus' teaching lessened respect for theirs. The Pharisees and scribes were his main opponents in Galilee.

In this chapter we shall study the accounts of five men who became disciples; five healings which were typical of the activity that convinced the crowds that Jesus' authority and power came from

God; and five occasions of conflict with the religious teachers.

1. The Challenge is Accepted: the First Five Disciples

(a) Andrew, Peter, James and John (Mark 1.16-20; Matt. 4.18-22; Luke 5.1-11)

There had to be someone prepared to carry on his work should Jesus be imprisoned or killed like John had been. We do not know how many disciples he had, nor the names of more than twelve or so, but these are probably typical of many who were attracted by his teaching and, even more, by the kind of man he was. The first disciples were possibly friends of John the Baptist who recognized Jesus as the one they had been preparing for and gave him their allegiance when John was shut up in Herod's fortress.

Andrew and his brother Simon, and the two sons of Zebedee, James and John, were fishermen. Jesus asked them to follow him, saying he would make them 'fishers of men'. Instead of working for themselves, they were henceforth to draw other men into the fellowship in which each could find his real self in helping others.

Luke says they had made an astonishing catch by following Jesus' directions to let down their nets in the deep water. There were so many fish that the nets were breaking and they had to call the second boat to help them. This gives the greater point to the promise : 'Follow me, and I will make you become fishers of men.' It brought Simon Peter to his knees in awe, begging Jesus to leave him alone – he was not worthy of this calling. Jesus told him not to be afraid. This story must have come from Peter. Probably he confided to a friend the impact that day had had on him, and years later it came to Luke's knowledge.

(b) Levi (Mark 2.13-17; Matt. 9.9-13; Luke 5.27-32)

There is only this one further account of the calling of a disciple in the synoptic gospels.

Levi was a tax collector. He appears to have changed his name later, because he is referred to in the Gospel according to Matthew as – Matthew! Probably Mark and Luke never knew of this change of name.

Levi and his friends were the cause of trouble between Jesus and the Pharisees. Tax collectors were despised for working for the hated Roman government. Contact with Gentiles made them ritually unclean, and they were avoided by strict Jews like the Pharisees and scribes. Many of them were dishonest, using their position to extort a little extra for themselves. They were thus 'sinners' on three counts: collaboration with the occupation government; the ritual 'sin' of defilement, and the actual sin of dishonesty.

Jesus knew that men are more likely to be sorry and want to change what is wrong in their lives if they have someone who trusts them and never gives up hope. He befriended Levi and others like him because they had so few friends, and none except men like themselves. He said: 'Those who are well have no need of a physician, but those who are sick.'

Matthew quotes Jesus' paraphrase of some words of the prophet Hosea: 'I desire mercy and not sacrifice.' Hosea had maintained that God wanted us to have 'steadfast love and the knowledge of God'. It was this more demanding religion of relationship with God and mercy towards one's fellow-men that Jesus expected. For him, a 'respectability' which despised others was not religion. The Pharisees, however, could not change, but Levi accepted the challenge and left his tax office and became a disciple.

2. The Response of the Crowds: Five Healings

(a) The man with the unclean spirit (Mark 1.21-8; Luke 4.31-7)

What we would today call mental illness was believed in the first century to be due to a spirit or demon taking possession of a man's mind. It was for those days a quite rational explanation of unusual behaviour. To the amazement of those present in the Capernaum synagogue one sabbath day, Jesus healed such a man. They exclaimed: 'What is this? A new teaching! With authority he commands even the unclean spirits, and they obey him.'

The deranged man shouted out that Jesus was 'the Holy One of God.' Mark tells of several occasions on which such men apparently recognized what the clever Pharisees could not: that the source of Jesus' healing power was God himself. Even though the conscious mind is severely disturbed, acute perception at a deeper level of consciousness is possible.[1]

(b) Simon Peter's mother-in-law (Mark 1.29-31; Matt. 8.14-15; Luke 4.38-9)

Peter's mother-in-law was healed of fever, and seemed to have none of the usual after-fever weakness because she was able to get up immediately and look after her guests. It may be that she had been anxious about the new life Peter was living and this had caused the fever; but when Jesus took her hand and lifted her up she realized that she need not worry about Peter's wandering around the countryside in his company.

Her response to healing was the disciple's response: 'she served them'. The response to receiving is to give to others – or should be. On another occasion Jesus told the twelve, 'You received without pay, give without pay' (Matt. 10.8).

(c) The leper (Mark 1.40-45; Matt. 8.1-4; Luke 5.12-16)

A leper was in a desperate situation in the first century. Not only was his disease disfiguring and disabling; he was driven out of his village by his neighbours' fear of catching it from him; and everyone thought that he must be to blame, that there must be some great secret sin in his life. In the first century sickness and sin were thought to be connected. 'Unclean' physically, socially and religiously, the leper was an outcast.

When a leper came up to Jesus asking 'If you will, you can make me clean', he was hoping for forgiveness as well as physical healing. That he even approached a healthy man is an indication of Jesus' reputation; lepers had to keep their distance: he must have heard that this man refused no one. Although told to say nothing, other than reporting his cure to the priests who had to witness it before he could return to normal life, he talked so freely that his benefactor could no longer enter a village without being mobbed.

---

[1] A psychiatrist says: 'I am aware that the man who is said to be deluded may be in his delusion telling me the truth, and this in no equivocal or metaphorical sense, but quite literally, and that the cracked mind of the schizophrenic may let in light which does not enter the intact minds of many sane people whose minds are closed.' (R. D. Laing, The Divided Self, Penguin Books, p.27.)

(d) The paralysed man (Mark 2.1-12; Matt. 9.1-8; Luke 5.17-26)

Jesus' growing fame brought Pharisees and scribes to see for themselves what lay behind the reports they had been hearing.

On one occasion his house at Capernaum was so crowded that four men who wished to bring a paralysed friend were forced to exercise their ingenuity and remove some of the roof-tiles and lower the stretcher at Jesus' feet. Such faith touched him.

Strangely, his first words were not of healing, but of forgiveness. Apparently he could tell that guilt was the cause of the man's paralysis. Psychiatrists today are familiar with cases of paralysis in which there is no damage to muscles or nerve endings: the cause seems not to be physical disease, but mental un-ease. Jesus did not treat the symptom (paralysis) only, but dealt with its cause; the man had to be mentally and spiritually 'whole' before he could be physically 'healthy'. The gift of the kingdom which he had come to bring on earth was spiritual wholeness as well as physical well-being.

The scribes were outraged to hear a man say such words as 'My son, your sins are forgiven.' Only God could forgive sins, and it was blasphemy to claim equality with God. Jesus used the man's healing to prove that he did have authority to forgive – God's authority.

The people were amazed and glorified God. This was something quite new in their experience.

(e) The man with a withered hand (Mark 3.1-6; Matt. 12.9-14; Luke 6.6-11)

On another sabbath, a man with a withered hand was in a synagogue where Jesus was present. Pharisees watched to see what he would do. There was a commandment that no work could be done on the sabbath, and they interpreted this to include the care of the sick; a doctor could attend a patient only if his life was in danger. Jesus queried whether this was a legitimate interpretation: 'Is it lawful on the sabbath to do good or to do harm, to save life or to kill?' God had given the commandment for man's benefit,[2] as a day of rest for slaves, servants, animals, everybody; but the Pharisees preferred their own interpretation, 'the traditions of the elders'. Jesus was grieved at their hardness of heart in the face of a fellow-

[2] See Mark 2.27 and Ex. 23.12.

man's suffering, and without regard to the consequences for himself he restored the man's hand.

Luke says it was his right hand. In that case the disability could have made it difficult for him to earn a living; most tools were made for right-handed use.

These five healings were typical of many more, as Mark indicates in his summary of the progress of Jesus' mission (3.7-12). Probably these were recorded because of the particular circumstances surrounding them; we shall see that two of these stories of healing also show the growing opposition to the new teaching.

3. The Challenge is Rejected: Five Stories of Conflict

(a) Blasphemy (Mark 2.1-12; Matt. 9.1-8; Luke 5.17-26)

Jesus was accused of blasphemy because he assured the paralysed man that his sins were forgiven.

His defence was that 'The Son of man has authority on earth to forgive sins' and proved that it was true by telling the man to pick up his stretcher and go home, although he had had to be carried there by four friends.

(b) Eating with sinners (Mark 2.13-17; Matt. 9.9-13; Luke 5.27-32)

He was criticized by the scribes for sharing a meal with tax collectors and sinners in Levi's house.

The reason he gave was 'I came not to call the righteous, but sinners.' In the Old Testament 'righteous' means 'to be in right relationships with'. God was 'righteous' because he cared for the widows and orphans and unjustly treated. The righteous God demanded 'righteousness' of his chosen people, that is, brotherly love and concern for one another. The 'righteous', those who were already living in right relationships with their fellows, were in less need of help than those who had become outcast from family, friends, society and, above all, God, whether through misfortune or sin. What Jesus wanted for them was, first, their repentance and desire to start a new life, and second, justice and acceptance from others to enable them to do it. He knew that they would gradually lose their feeling of inferiority and insecurity once they were accepted into a fellowship which valued them for their own sakes;

and would then no longer need to resort to anti-social behaviour to gain recognition.

(c) The disciples' disregard of the fasting rules (Mark 2.18-22; Matt. 9.14-17; Luke 5.33-9)

Why were his disciples not keeping the usual fasting rules of Judaism?

Jesus' answer was two-fold. First, he pointed out that the custom of fasting was suspended for wedding guests while the bridegroom was still with them. A wedding feast had often been used as a symbol of the messianic banquet which was to usher in the age of messiah. By implication, he was the 'bridegroom' and the messianic age had begun. Secondly, he said that new cloth cannot be used to patch an old garment, it merely tears it further. Nor can old wineskins contain the potent, fermenting new wine.

These metaphors suggest that he saw his teaching as incompatible with the traditions he was accused of breaking.

There is no doubt that Jesus respected Judaism. He went to the temple for the great feasts and regularly to the synagogue like any good Jew. But he believed that love of God must show itself in concern for the welfare of his people, and that this took precedence over a rigid rule-keeping. He was thus a threat to the Pharisees and scribes to whom such rules had become the most important thing in life.

(d) Working on the sabbath (Mark 2.23-8; Matt. 12.1-8; Luke 6.1-5)

The Pharisees accused his disciples of working on the sabbath because they had picked a few ears of grain to eat while walking through the fields.

Again Jesus' defence was two-fold. First, that David's men had eaten even the holy bread when there was no other food for the priest to give them,[3] and second (and this is in Matthew only), that priests work on the sabbath without profaning it and 'something greater than the temple is here' (Matt. 12.5-6). His authority for the stand he is taking is summed up in 'The Son of man is lord even of the sabbath.'

---

[3] I Samuel 21.1-6.

(e) Healing on the sabbath (Mark 3.1-6; Matt. 12.9-14; Luke 6.6-11)

The fifth occasion of conflict which Mark has recorded is the sabbath healing of the man with the withered hand which we have already studied.

The Pharisees could give no answer to the question put to them. They could not say that the purpose of the sabbath was to do harm; but neither could they answer that it was to do good because that is exactly what they were objecting to Jesus' doing. Healing an incapacitated man was doing good and, if he had difficulty in earning a living, it could also be saving life – his own or his children's.

What they did do was discuss with the Herodians[4] how they could get rid of the troublemaker. He was a threat to their treasured beliefs and customs. His popularity was weakening their own prestige in the eyes of the people. The authority with which he acted and spoke could not but raise a question as to the real basis of theirs.

The Pharisees must have been exceedingly angry to have considered joining forces with the Herodians; the incident at Herod's birthday party is some indication of the standards of Herod's friends. The Pharisees were good men on the whole; they would not normally have associated with Herodians.

REVISION QUESTIONS

1. Describe the circumstances in which Jesus used the expression 'fishers of men'. What meaning do you think it would have had for the first disciples?

2. Tell in detail the story of the paralysed man. Discuss the significance of the conversations.

3. What were the causes of hostility to Jesus in Galilee? How did he justify his actions and attitude?

4. Draw a sketch map of Palestine and mark in the places from which the crowds mentioned in Mark 3.7-8 came. (Add to your map as you come across other place names in the synoptic gospels.)

[4] See the section in chapter 1 on 'Historical and Political Situation'.

7 *The Men of the Kingdom*

Mark 3.13-19; 6.7-16; 8.34-8 and
parallel passages

On one occasion Jesus said that those who were close to him, like members of his own family, were those who did the will of God (Mark 3.31-5). He wanted such friends to help him, for he could see that those who flocked to hear him speak or to seek healing of mind or body were 'harassed and helpless, like sheep without a shepherd'. He said to his disciples 'The harvest is plentiful, but the labourers are few; pray therefore the Lord of the harvest to send out labourers into his harvest' (Matt. 9.37-8).

In this chapter we shall see how Jesus chose and trained a few men for a more responsible sharing in his mission to all men. They were warned that their lives would not be easy; they would be persecuted as he had been. But discipleship would bring its own rewards: 'Blessed are the eyes which see what you see! For I tell you that many prophets and kings desired to see what you see, and did not see it, and to hear what you hear, and did not hear it' (Luke 10.23-4).

From the knowledge we have we can see that Jesus did not chose those he did for their cleverness or goodness. Levi had a bad reputation, James and John Zebedee looked for privilege for themselves, Peter consistently acted without thinking, and Judas Iscariot could never have really understood the master he followed. Jesus must have thought they could be strengthened by sharing his life and relationship with God, and so in time become a strength to others.

1. Choosing the Twelve

Mark 3.13-19; Matt. 9.35—10.4; Luke 6.12-16

After spending the night alone in the hills in prayer, he chose twelve of his disciples, and gave them authority to share in his work of teaching and healing. The fact that there were twelve, the number of the tribes of Israel, suggests that he thought of them as the leaders of a new Israel, the kingdom of God which he and they together were to inaugurate on earth.

Two reasons had been given for calling the first disciples: their own needs (Mark 2.17), and the needs of others (Mark 1.17). This twofold nature of Christian discipleship: personal fulfilment through a life lived close to God and in loving relationship with one another, and concern for other men and women, again appears in the account of the choosing of the twelve. They were 'to be with him' and were 'to be sent out to preach and have authority to cast out demons' (Mark 3.14). That is, they were first to share his life, and then his care for the unhappy, the outcast, and the sick.

The twelve names are not identical in all three gospels. Matthew and Mark list a Thaddeus, while Luke has Judas the son of James (as well as Judas Iscariot, the Judas who later betrayed Jesus). Probably by the time the gospels were written an evangelist well-known in a particular area had been confused with one of the original twelve. They were Simon (also known as Peter), Andrew, James and John Zebedee, Philip, Bartholomew, Matthew, Thomas, James (son of Alphaeus), Simon (sometimes called the Zealot and sometimes the Canaanite), Judas Iscariot, and either Thaddeus or Judas the son of James.

2. The Mission of the Twelve

Mark 6.7-16; Matt. 10.5-16; Luke 9.1-6

The word 'disciple' means a learner, but not only of theoretical knowledge; he is one who learns by putting into practice the principles of his teacher. The twelve are often referred to as disciples, but are also distinguished from the larger group of those learning from Jesus' life and words by the name 'apostle'. Luke says that Jesus named them apostles (6.13). The word means 'one who is sent out as a messenger with power to act for the sender'. They had been given a share in his authority,[1] and were to continue his work of bringing God's love to men so that all would want to accept his sovereignty in their own lives.

As still today in Hindu and Buddhist countries, wandering holy men would have been a familiar sight in first-century Palestine. On their first mission they were to take no food, money, or begging-bag, but be dependent on those they helped. They were to wear only the one tunic, and not carry the usual travellers' cloak which did duty as a blanket at night. They were not to be a burden on those who gave them hospitality, but to stay in one house only in each village, and to go straight through any village where they were not wanted. Their mission, that is, the purpose for which they were sent out (from the Latin missio=a sending), was to heal, to preach repentance, and to announce that 'the kingdom of heaven is at hand'. It was thus like Jesus' own.

One strange result of this first mission of the twelve apostles was that Herod believed that John the Baptist must have come back from the dead! Surely what they were witnessing was the fulfilment of his proclamation: 'the kingdom of heaven is at hand'.

Matthew tells us that they were told to go only to 'the lost sheep of the house of Israel' and not to Samaritans or Gentiles. Elsewhere Matthew reports Jesus as saying 'I was sent only to the lost sheep of the house of Israel' (15.24). But Jesus never seemed to make any distinction in his dealings with people of different races; perhaps Matthew did not want to include anything in his gospel which would prejudice conservative Palestinians who themselves had nothing to do with Gentiles. It is only in the Gospel of Matthew that such sayings are found.

3. The Mission of the Seventy

Luke 10.1-20

Luke reports the mission of a party of seventy. They went to areas where Jesus himself intended later to visit; they were to prepare the way. Their instructions were similar to those of the twelve.

They returned delighted with the success of their efforts: 'Lord,

[1] Mark 6.7; Matt. 10.1; Luke 9.1. See also Matt. 10.40

even the demons are subject to us in your name!' It is obvious from the imaginative symbolism of Jesus' reply, 'I saw Satan fall like lightning from heaven', that he saw this successful beginning to the kingdom as a death-blow to the power of evil. However, he put their natural elation into proper perspective by reminding them that the real cause for rejoicing was that 'your names are written in heaven' – that their work had eternal significance and value.

Matthew and Mark do not mention the mission of the seventy. This number symbolized, in the ancient world, the Gentile nations, and 'the seventy' may have had for Luke's readers the same significance which 'the twelve' had for those of Israelite descent: the kingdom which Jesus proclaimed was for the whole world, not only for Israel. Luke, however, mentions both tours. Perhaps when Jesus wanted the apostles with him for further instructions he sent out the larger group. There may have been many more such group-missions; the evangelists naturally recorded only what was necessary to make clear to their particular readers the relevance and meaning of the gospel for them.

4. The Fate of Disciples

Matt. 10.16-42; Mark 8.34-8

Jesus knew that his followers would not always be so well-received or successful. He warned that they would sometimes be like 'sheep in the midst of wolves'; yet their own attitude was always to be, at the one and the same time, intelligently fearless, loving, and un-embittered: 'so be wise as serpents and innocent as doves'. It was inevitable that their reception would be mixed, as his had been: welcomed by many, but rejected by others, and those often the most powerful in the land.

When they were accused unjustly, or imprisoned, they were not to worry, 'for what you are to say will be given you in that hour; for it is not you who speak, but the Spirit of your Father speaking through you' (Matt. 10.17-33).

Their discipleship would even cause division within families. Within one family there could be both acceptance of the gospel and rejection, one member following him while another attacked him. Though it was far from his intention or desire he could foresee that his message of love would bring not peace but a sword – at least for a time (Matt. 10.34-6).

He never tried to hide the fact that full discipleship – acceptance of the reign of God in one's life – was totally demanding. It could mean putting response to him before family ties. It might bring suffering. The surrender that it asked of them would seem at first a kind of death, like his acceptance of the cross, because it is inevitable that men must lose their old self-centred lives before they are able to find in a generous self-giving their real and authentic 'self' (Matt. 10.37-9; Mark 8.34-5). He wanted them to be able to make the complete commitment asked of a disciple with their eyes wide open to all that was involved.

He identified himself with them, and their mission with his own : those who received them, received both him and the Father who had sent him (Matt. 10.40-42). Discipleship of the Christ was the way to a living relationship with God.

5. Rejection by Men – Acceptance by God
Matt. 11.12-30; Luke 7.31-5; 10.13-22

Jesus had been disappointed with the response to John's and his own preaching in Galilee. He likened his generation to sulky children who will not join in any game suggested : they had criticized John's asceticism over food and drink, and his own enjoyment of a meal with men they called sinners. He thought it quite likely that the Gentile towns of Tyre and Sidon would have made a more ready response than Capernaum and the other Galilean towns where most of his mighty works had been done. These had brought judgment on themselves by their refusal of the chance for a new and fuller life (Matt. 11.12-24).

At the same time, he rejoiced that the truth was understood by ordinary men and women, 'babes', to the worldly-wise. He invited 'all who labour and are heavy laden' – the anxious and strained – to find new peace and renewed strength in him. His conviction that 'all things have been delivered to me by my Father' enabled him, with utter confidence, to call others to share in his life of Sonship (Matt. 11.25-30).

REVISION QUESTIONS

1. Why did Jesus choose the apostles? What significance did the number twelve have for them?

2. Give his instructions to the twelve in detail. What do you think was the point of their 'poverty' – their few possessions, and their dependence on those they visited while preaching and healing? How does the picture this gives compare with the church today?

3. Write brief notes on the following:
disciple; apostle; mission; righteous; kingdom (translating the Greek *basileia*); losing your life in order to find it; ritual defilement. (Those that are not mentioned in this chapter can be revised by looking up chapter 6.3(b) (righteous); chapter 5.2 (ritual defilement); chapter 4.2 (kingdom).)

4. What treatment could a disciple of Jesus expect, and why? Is it any different today, not only in your own country but in the world generally?

8 The Parables of the Kingdom

Mark 3.22-4—4.34 and parallel passages

The parables are Jesus' most characteristic teaching. Our word 'parable' comes from the Greek *parabolē* (*para* = by the side of, and *ballō* = throw or place). A parable is a comparison of what is well-known with what is strange, in the hope that by a sudden flash of insight one will grasp intuitively what could not be taught directly. Jesus used parables to try to reveal to men something of the hidden and mysterious ways of God.

Unlike an allegory, in which each separate point in the story stands for something else, a parable has just one point and it is meant to be taken as a whole. This one point may, of course, 'speak' differently to different people. Some of the parables in the synoptic gospels have had an allegorical interpretation added to them, but it is not part of the original parable.

Jesus described the kingdom of God in similes and metaphors drawn from everyday Palestinian life. The very oddness of the comparison is meant to set one thinking, and when the analogy comes clear the sudden, fresh perception challenges one's whole attitude to life. His parables have never lost their value, despite our quite different environment from that of first-century Palestinians to whom they were addressed. We do, however, have to see them against that environment.

The five parables which Mark records at this point in his gospel would have reassured the men of the kingdom of the ultimate success of their efforts – necessary encouragement to that handful of uneducated fishermen, faced with the incredibly difficult task of spreading the news of God's love in Roman-occupied Palestine.

1. *Parable of the Strong Man*

Mark 3.22-30; Matt. 12-24-32; Luke 11.15-23

Jesus was accused of casting out demons by the power of the prince of demons, Beelzebul. The parable of the strong man showed how illogical such an accusation was. Would Satan cast out his own evil spirits and make the possessed man well again? No; the fact that Jesus can heal a 'possessed' man is proof that the power of evil has been broken. 'If it is by the Spirit of God that I cast out demons, then the kingdom of God has come upon you' (Matt. 12.28). No evil spirit possessed him; he is the strong man because he is empowered by God. To say otherwise is the unforgiveable sin of blasphemy against the Spirit; unforgiveable, because a man who refuses to recognize good when he sees it has put himself beyond the possibility of help. To choose to deny good, is to choose evil, and the good is then powerless to help you.

2. *Parable of the Sower*

Mark 4.1-9; Matt. 13.1-9; Luke 8.4-8

In first-century Palestine seed was scattered by hand as the sower walked up and down the field. Only after the sowing were the fields ploughed so that the earth was turned up to cover the seed.

A wooden plough did not always manage to break up the path which the villagers had trodden hard as they took a short-cut across the fallow fields, and seed which had fallen on it was eaten by birds.

Seed which fell on soil that only just covered the rocky substrata could not put down deep roots, and the young plants soon withered and died.

The seeds which had been blown under the thorn-bushes separating one field from the next could not compete for the moisture and nourishment they needed, and also died.

So much seed yielded no return. Yet the farmer knew that he would still have a good harvest, perhaps thirty, sixty, or even a hundred times the weight of the seed he had sown.

This is a true picture of the hazards of indiscriminate sowing. Jesus' disciples could be reassured that they too might expect a like yield from their equally indiscriminate sowing of the word of the gospel. Others who heard this parable might find themselves forced to ask if they would be part of the 'harvest': had they let the seed of God's word grow in their hearts?

An interpretation of the parable of the sower has turned it into an allegory in which Jesus is the sower of the word, which is received with varying response, but when it is accepted in the good soil of a receptive heart the yield is a hundredfold (Mark 4.13-20; Matt. 13.18-23; Luke 8.11-15).

What is the purpose of this interpretation? Why would Jesus use a parable if he had to interpret it by an allegory? Perhaps what we have here is a sermon of the early church which became attached to the original parable during the oral period of the gospel, in which the falling away of some Christians from their first enthusiastic acceptance of the gospel is described in terms of the parable of the sower. Alternatively, it may be an attempt by a preacher to puzzle out why some accept the reign of God in their hearts, allowing him to transform their lives creatively, while others reject it. In either case the teaching is the same as that of the parable, reassurance of the ultimate success of the evangelists' mission.

3. Parable of the Lamp
Mark 4.21-5; Luke 8.16-18

Jesus had lit a lamp which must go on revealing God's love. Nothing in the gospel was to be kept secret; all that the disciples had received they were to share with others and in doing so they would find themselves further enriched: 'the measure you give will be the measure you get'.

This parable might well challenge Pharisees to consider whether they had been right to exclude Gentiles from the revelation of God which had been entrusted to Israel.

(There is a strange passage in Mark 4.10-12; Matt. 13.10-15; Luke 8.9-10, in which Jesus is asked his reason for speaking in parables. Again, we seem to have evidence of puzzlement: why could some understand Jesus' teaching as the best way for human beings to live, and others apparently just not understand – or at least not accept it? It may be that the disciples thought Jesus was deliberately hiding his inner meaning from some people. Jesus himself undoubtedly used parables because they would reveal to all levels of intelligence and education the spiritual mysteries of life; see for example Mark 4.33-4 and Matt. 13.34-5.)

4. Parable of the Seed Growing Secretly
Mark 4.26-9

The kingdom is like the grain which germinates and grows and ripens without further effort by the farmer after sowing. Again, this would reassure disciples who saw little outward response to their teaching. It may also have warned the Zealots who wanted to end the Roman occupation and restore the kingdom of Israel by force: the true kingdom of God could never be brought about by force; it grows quietly and hiddenly in each receptive individual's heart.

The ripe grain awaiting the sickle recalls Jesus' words about the harvest just before he chose the twelve. The words of the prophets through the centuries had been the seed; now, with him present, the harvest into the kingdom can begin. It is by personal response to him that men are saved.

5. Parable of the Mustard Seed
Mark 4.30-32; Matt. 13.31-2; Luke 13.18-19

Just as the mustard seed which, although the smallest of seeds, can grow into a shrub six to twelve feet high so that birds can build their nests in it, so also the small band of disciples will become in time a great fellowship in which men of all nations may find a home.

Five centuries before Christ, Ezekiel had used similar imagery to reassure the exiles in Babylon that they would not only return to Jerusalem but that a new nation, attracting men of all races, would one day spring from its soil.[1] Jesus' hearers were all familiar with the Hebrew scriptures and would have known Ezekiel's message of hope; now they could see that the kingdom which they were helping to build was its fulfilment.

[1] Ezekiel 17.22-4.

48

In such ways Jesus built up the confidence of the men of the kingdom: however few they were, God was working with them.

REVISION QUESTIONS

1. Recount the parable of the sower in detail. What other parables have similar teaching about the ultimate success of the kingdom of God?

2. What is the purpose of a parable?

3. Discuss the purpose for which the interpretation of the parable of the sower might have been used. Why is it unlikely to have been Jesus' own words?

9 The 'Mighty Works': Signs of the Kingdom

Mark 4.35—6.56 and parallel passages

Jesus of Nazareth taught not only in words, but also by the way he lived and the things he did. Much of his activity was outside the normal experience and expectation of men, and met with astonished awe. We have seen how the men in the Capernaum synagogue exclaimed 'What is this? A new teaching! With authority he commands even the unclean spirits, and they obey him' (Mark 1.21-8). When he healed the paralysed man by forgiving him those present 'were all amazed and glorified God, saying, "We never saw anything like this"' (Mark 2.1-12). Luke's comment is that 'the power of the Lord was with him to heal' (5.17).

The Hebrew scriptures, which we call the Old Testament, spoke of Yahweh's power in the creation-process. They held that the same power lay behind the disasters which overtook Israel when it forgot the covenant obligations of loyalty to Yahweh and brotherliness to one another. The psalmists spoke of Yahweh holding the raging seas in check. He worked miracles through chosen and dedicated men like Elijah and Elisha. Yahweh's power was the source of all other power in the universe. The Greek word for this power of God's was *dunamis*.

When men recognized that it was God's power at work in Jesus' healings, they spoke of them as *dunameis*, acts of (God's) power. They saw that they could change a man's life: Levi's, the leper's, that of the man with the withered hand. His healings were acts of love, with an effect like dynamite on a society which was indifferent to the suffering it was incapable of ending. His exorcisms of the destructive spirits possessing men's minds were evidence that his *dunameis* were more powerful than evil. They did not speak of wonders, which is what we often mean by the word 'miracle'; Jesus always refused to work wonders which would compel men to believe. They spoke instead of his 'mighty works': signs of the dynamic difference God's kingdom of love could make to all human existence if men would accept his sovereignty in their hearts and minds. Our words dynamo, dynamite, dynamic, come from the same Greek root as *dunameis* which has been translated in the Revised Standard Version (RSV) of the Bible as 'mighty works'.

1. *Calming the Storm*

Mark 4.35-41; Matt. 8.23-7; Luke 8.22-5

One evening Jesus and his disciples were crossing Lake Galilee when a sudden storm threatened to swamp the boat. To the first-century fishermen, so vulnerable to the forces of nature in their small boats, the frequent, violent storms of Lake Galilee must have seemed like a demon trying to destroy them.

The word 'rebuked' is the same word Jesus used when driving evil spirits from men. To the disciples, he was 'exorcising' the destructive demon in the storm, and consequently taking away their fear. Who could he be, who possessed a power which their forefathers had believed belonged only to God?

... they cried to the Lord in their trouble,
and he delivered them from their distress;
he made the storm be still,
and the waves of the sea were hushed. *Ps.* 107.28-9 (RSV)

2. *The Gerasene Demoniac*

Mark 5.1-20; Matt. 8.28-34; Luke 8.26-39

Jesus had calmed the forces of nature which threatened to destroy the disciples. Now he is shown bringing order and peace into the mind of a man who was destroying himself.

The mad man had abnormal strength. He terrorized the neighbourhood and was a danger to himself. It must have seemed to his deranged mind that an army of voices and conflicting tensions drove him on, for his name for himself was Legion – 'for we are many'. He approached Jesus, as if he had sensed his power to help. The Decapolis (literally, 'the ten towns') was a Gentile area to the south-east of Galilee; the gospel was already being taken into the wider world. The location of 'the country of the Gerasenes' is now unknown. The presence of pigs suggests a Gentile area. The sick man's expression, 'Son of the Most High God', and his return to the Decapolis, suggest that he may himself have been a Gentile.

The report of the stampeding pigs is a strange feature of this story. Unclean animals would have seemed to the evangelists an appropriate vehicle for the destruction of the legion of unclean spirits; but it is unlikely that Jesus did anything that would have caused their death. It may be that a local story of a landslide which took with it a herd of grazing pigs has become mixed up with the healing of a mad man in the same district, and Mark and the others have accepted it without further thought.

3. *The Woman with a Haemorrhage*
Mark 5.25-34; Matt. 9.20-22; Luke 8.43-8

This healing is sandwiched between the two halves of the story of Jairus' daughter which we shall study next. Jesus was on his way to Jairus' house, and a great crowd of townspeople thronged about the party. A woman who had had a haemorrhage for twelve years came up behind him and, under cover of the crowd, touched his clothes as if she thought there was something magic in the contact to heal her. However, once she had spoken openly about her trouble and despair Jesus was able to assure her that it was faith that had made her well, not magic, and she could go in peace, confident of her cure.

The Hebrews had long believed that 'life' was in the blood; after all, an animal bled to death. For this Hebrew woman, losing blood was losing life; and not only in the physical sense, because she was regarded as ritually unclean while she continued haemorrhaging and consequently cut off from the religion of her people. Jesus had, in fact, restored her to a life worth living.

4. Jairus' Daughter

Mark 5.21-43; Matt. 9.18-26; Luke 8.40-56

Jesus then continued his journey to Jairus' daughter. It is impossible to know if she were 'medically dead' or, as Jesus himself inferred, in a coma or deeply unconscious state. Jairus was an official representative of the religion of Judaism. Though Jesus met with opposition from Pharisees and scribes, and another synagogue ruler was indignant when he healed on the sabbath[1] there were others who were not opposed to what he was doing among the people. The messenger from Jairus' household had been most courteous in calling him 'teacher', for example. Jesus may well have had hopes of speaking to the whole Jewish nation through Jairus, and of assuring them that he had not come to destroy what was of eternal value in their religion. 'Do not fear, only believe' may have been meant for more ears than Jairus' alone!

It is also possible that there is a deeper significance in his words about the little girl. The Sadducees did not believe in any form of existence after the death of the body; this was one of the points on which they were divided from the Pharisees.[2] Jesus may have been speaking to them through Jairus' daughter: 'The child is not dead but sleeping', saying, in effect, that death is not the end. In the two synoptic gospel accounts of Jesus giving life to those believed dead[3] identical words are used: 'I say to you, arise.'

By calming the storm Jesus took away the fear of death. He restored the Gerasene demoniac's 'dead' reason. The woman with the haemorrhage had been saved from a living death. Now he has given back life to a young girl. These four mighty works are saying that this man has power to give peace and hope and new life to those with faith. The fifth points forward to the future, when the Christian community after Jesus' death found that his life was available to them in the 'breaking of bread'.

---

[1] Luke 13.10-17. See chapter 17.3(b).
[2] For a discussion of the differences between Pharisees and Sadducees see the section on 'Social and Religious Situation' in chapter 1.
[3] The other report is in Luke 7.11-17. See chapter 17.3(a).

5. The Feeding of the Five Thousand and the Walking on the Water

Mark 6.30-56; Matt. 14.13-36; Luke 9.10-17

When the twelve returned from their mission Jesus had wanted to take them away to a quiet place to rest and think out the implications of their new experiences. But a crowd pursued them even to the isolated spot he had chosen. It grew late, and the disciples wanted him to send the people away to get food. All they had themselves was five loaves and two fish. Jesus told the people to sit down on the grass. He then took the loaves and the fish, blessed and broke them, and gave them to the disciples to set before the people as if this was another lesson in discipleship: they were to feed his people.

There was no expression of astonishment or awe at what seems the most stupendous of his mighty works! We are merely told that the disciples got into their boat to cross to Bethsaida while Jesus dismissed the crowd and then went into the hills to pray. About 3 a.m. they were terrified to see a figure coming towards the boat over the water, until Jesus' voice reassured them: 'Take heart, it is I; have no fear.' What is the significance of these two incidents?

Firstly, the repetition of Jesus' four actions at the Last Supper when he took, blessed, broke, and gave the bread with the words: 'This is my body', suggest that the meaning of what took place in the lonely countryside lies in its relationship with the Lord's Supper of the breaking of bread,[4] which by the time the gospels were written had long been the church's act of worship.

Secondly, the twelve baskets of left-over fragments suggest that it was not merely a miraculous picnic meal for 5,000 but an invitation to the twelve tribes, to all Israel.

Thirdly, the hungry 'sheep without a shepherd' in the 'lonely place' (notice how many times it is so described so that we shall begin to ask its significance) recalls the hungry Hebrews in the uninhabited wilderness before they entered the promised land. There Moses was led by God to find the manna with which to feed them.[5]

The evangelists must surely have meant their readers to see that

[4] Mark 14.22-5. See chapter 13.1.   [5] Ex. 16.

54

God was now feeding his people through his servant Jesus: the long-awaited 'messianic banquet' which would inaugurate the kingdom of God was the Lord's Supper, the communion service of the Christian community and covenant meal of the new Israel through which all could share in the life of the risen Lord. The words of Jesus recorded in Matthew 14.27-31 would reassure his followers down the ages.

REVISION QUESTIONS

1. Describe in detail all that happened when Jesus cured a man in the country of the Gerasenes. How would we speak of his illness today?

2. Give a full account of what happened after Jairus met Jesus. What do these incidents teach of the significance of Jesus' mighty works?

3. Recount the story of the feeding of the five thousand. Several features of Mark's account suggest a deeper meaning. Comment on these features.

4. Write brief notes on the Greek word *dunameis*; rebuked (as used in Mark 4.39 and 1.25); Decapolis; Legion (as used in Mark 5.9); and the meaning and possible significance of the Aramaic expression '*Talitha cumi*' (Mark 5.41).

10 *Outside Galilee*

Mark 7.1—8.21 and parallel passages

The time came for the mission to extend outside Galilee. Already there had been signs of interest in the new teaching from Idumea, Judea and the Decapolis in the south, and from around Tyre and Sidon in the north (Mark 3.7-8; 5.20); now Jesus would travel in these areas. Was he forced to leave Galilee by the opposition he had aroused in influential quarters? Or was his only reason the desire to bring the kingdom of God within reach of the greatest possible number of people?

This chapter begins and ends with the Pharisees questioning Jesus. Their attitude is in striking contrast to the response of the Gentiles he met.

1. *Pharisees and Scribes from Jerusalem*

Mark 7.1-23; Matt. 15.1-20

It is some indication of Jesus' growing reputation that Pharisees and scribes travelled north from Jerusalem to see for themselves. These two groups seemed constantly to be looking for grounds for criticism. Just before his departure from Galilee their complaint was that his disciples broke the traditions of the elders by not washing their hands before eating. For them, this was not a matter of hygiene, but of religion.

Jesus answered by a counter-attack: they put the traditions of men before the commandments of God. The example he gave was of the practice of *corban*, pledging one's money to God (that is, promising it to the temple). A man could then evade his responsibility for helping his parents financially by saying that his money was *corban*; but he was breaking the commandment to honour father and mother.

He then turned to the people to explain the difference between real sin and ritual taboos connected with food. The latter marked them off as different from their neighbours, and helped to preserve the unity of the clan or tribal group. In time these taboos came to be regarded as religious rites, as something required by their god. Observance by every member of the tribe was enforced by rigorous penalties for the smallest violation. They came to think that the safety and well-being of all was dependent on the correct perform-ance of the ritual. The Pharisees genuinely believed that Judaism's traditions were a necessary and important part of the worship of Yahweh and that Jesus' teaching endangered the whole nation of Israel.

He tried to explain that a man could not be defiled by anything he ate, nor could ritual washing remove the barriers that kept him from God. The sin which makes a man unclean comes only from within himself: his own evil thoughts and deeds (Mark 7.17-23). Jesus' teaching was revolutionary for his time, but it was a most necessary step in freeing men from the tribal and national and religious taboos which separate them from other groups.

2. *The Syro-Phoenician Woman's Daughter*
Mark 7.24-30; Matt. 15.21-8

Jesus began his travels outside Galilee by going first to the region of Tyre and Sidon in the north-west. These seaports were in Phoenicia and in the Roman province of Syria, hence the description of the woman whose daughter Jesus healed as 'Syro-Phoenician'. Matthew refers to her by the older name of 'Canaanite'. Apparently she followed the Greek religious ideas. She was not a Jew, either by birth or religion. He tested her motive in coming to him; did she regard him as just another wonder-working healer, or had she the faith which understood the message behind his healings?

The woman's reply revealed the insight which faith alone could have given her. Although she recognized that his first responsibility was to his own people, the Jews, she knew that his mission transcended national and racial barriers, and that the gifts of the kingdom were for all, whatever their racial origin.

This story would have been of great value as the gospel spread after Jesus' death. Those who had never known the Lord in his earthly life could be assured of his power to cast out of their lives anything that kept them from wholeness; it was not necessary to see his face, faith was the medium of contact.

Jesus' comparison of Tyre and Sidon with some of the Galilean villages was being proved true.[1]

3. The Deaf and Dumb Man of the Decapolis
Mark 7.31-7

From Tyre and Sidon Jesus travelled south to the Decapolis area. There he healed a man's deafness and enabled him to speak clearly. Although he said to tell no one, 'the more zealously they proclaimed it' as fulfilling Isaiah's prophecy of the messianic blessings; perhaps this passage from Isaiah 35.4-6 was in their minds:

> Say to those who are of a fearful heart,
>   'Be strong, fear not!
> Behold, your God will come with vengeance,
>   With the recompense of God.
>   He will come and save you.'
> Then the eyes of the blind shall be opened,
>   and the ears of the deaf unstopped;
> then shall the lame man leap like a hart,
> and the tongue of the dumb sing for joy.

There are several unusual features in this healing. It was done deliberately in private; the techniques of the popular faith-healers were used: saliva, touching, the looking to heaven as if to bring down divine power, words which expressed the cure desired, 'open' ears and tongue. Mark even tells us the Aramaic word which Jesus used, *Ephphatha*, 'be opened'. Are we to understand this healing as an acted parable of discipleship – even of Gentile discipleship – to the Greek world?

[1] Chapter 7.5.

The disciples had been taken apart from the crowds to hear all that Jesus' mission involved. When their ears were 'opened' to the full meaning of discipleship they were to 'speak plainly' what they had learnt, 'zealously proclaiming' the good news that the day of the Lord had come. In the next chapter we shall study two healings of blind men which might also be acted parables of discipleship. The mighty works spoke of life in the kingdom, no less than the parables.

4. The Feeding of the Four Thousand
Mark 8.1-10; Matt. 15.32-9

Once again a crowd gathered in an out of the way place. They stayed with Jesus three days and had no more food and were hungry. Some had 'come a long way'; he could not send them home hungry because they might faint on the way. The disciples were worried how they could get sufficient bread to feed such a crowd 'in the desert'. They had only seven loaves and a few small fish.

Jesus took, blessed, broke, and gave the bread to the disciples to set before the people, and then the fish. About four thousand ate and were satisfied. Seven baskets of left-over fragments were collected. As in the accounts of the feeding of the five thousand we are not told of any expression of astonishment at what had taken place.

Were there two separate occasions on which Jesus fed a large crowd? Luke does not record the feeding of the four thousand; has Mark, followed by Matthew, heard two slightly different versions of the one incident? Or is there a special significance in the numbers mentioned?

Just as the twelve baskets recalled Israel's twelve tribes so seven might represent the Gentiles[2] who had 'come a long way', that is, from right outside Israel, to share the covenant meal of the new Israel. Seven was the perfect number that signified completion. Perhaps we are to see in its use here an invitation to all mankind; there is sufficient of this food for all.

---

[2] The first Gentiles to hold official positions in the church were seven deacons (Acts 6.1-6); compare Luke's mission of the seventy, chapter 7.3.

5. The Pharisees ask for a Sign from Heaven

Mark 8.11-21; Matt. 16.1-12; 12.38-42; Luke 11.16,29

This chapter began with the Pharisees' criticism that the disciples did not observe the traditions of the elders. Now we see them asking Jesus for a sign from heaven to test the source of his power.

They were unwilling, or unable, to come to a definite decision about his authority. Ordinary people had welcomed the mighty works as evidence that the Day of the Lord had come at last. But the professionally trained religious leaders were reluctant to accept that a carpenter from an obscure village, with no rabbinic education, could be God's agent and the glorious messiah their ancestors had worshipped from afar. They therefore asked for some sign that would prove beyond all doubt that he was the messiah. Jesus refused.[3] He had always refused the kind of publicity which would have treated his *dunameis* as wonders compelling belief. Like the God he had come to reveal, he left men free to choose. For those who had ears to hear and eyes to see (the spiritual perception of faith) there had already been sufficient evidence that God was at work in the world through him.

Yet even the disciples had not understood when he broke the bread (Mark 8.21). Old Israel, represented by the Pharisees and scribes, would not recognize its messiah; the men of the new Israel did not yet see the significance of their new covenant meal. They were all still blind.

REVISION QUESTIONS

1. What were the causes of conflict between Jesus and the Pharisees? Describe one occasion when hostility was openly shown towards him, and one occasion when he showed his hostility towards their views.

2. Describe one healing where a relative came to Jesus on behalf of the sufferer. What part did faith play in such a healing?

3. If you had been present when Jesus was asked for 'a sign from

---

[3] 'The sign of the prophet Jonah' of Matt. 12.39; 16.4 and Luke 11.29 seems to be an allusion to the resurrection. It was the final and greatest of 'the mighty works' which were the sign of God's activity in his world through Jesus Christ.

heaven', how would you have explained that there had already been sufficient signs for those who had eyes to see?

4. What events that you have so far studied could be regarded as fulfilling the prophecy in Isaiah 35.4-6?

11 *The Mission Approaches its Climax: the Nature of True Discipleship*

Mark 8.22—10.52 and parallel passages

Accompanied by the disciples, Jesus set out for Jerusalem. The incidents of the journey which Mark reports have all to do with 'seeing', and the consequences of 'believing'. There was, first, the meeting at Bethsaida with the blind man to whom sight came only gradually; then Peter's insight at Caesarea Philippi; the vision on the Mount of Transfiguration; the realization that discipleship brings responsibility towards others and that power to fulfil it is to be sought in prayer; and, finally, the healing at Jericho of blind Bartimaeus whose immediate response as soon as he 'saw' was to follow Jesus on the way to Jerusalem, the place of death – but also of new life.

1. *The Blind Man at Bethsaida*
Mark 8.22-6

The man was brought to Jesus. He led him away from the village as he had the deaf mute,[1] and touched his eyes with saliva. Sight was partially restored: he could see men, but so indistinctly that they looked like tree-trunks walking. The man would of course have known the shape of tree-trunks by touch; what he now saw moved, like men, but were shapeless, like trees. Jesus again laid his hands on the man's eyes, and he 'saw everything clearly', just as the deaf mute had been able to 'speak plainly'.

This is the only account in the synoptic gospels of a healing done

[1] Chapter 10.3.

in stages. Did Jesus not have the power to heal this man outright as he had others? Or is it another acted parable, by which we are to see that full understanding of the gospel comes only gradually? The Pharisees wanted proof beyond all doubt. The disciples did not understand Jesus' vocation in the way he himself did. Yet, by journeying in his company, the faith that 'sees' and responds would grow.

2. Caesarea Philippi
Mark 8.27—9.1; Matt. 16.13-28; Luke 9.18-27

The city of Caesarea Philippi is to the north of Galilee. It had been rebuilt by the tetrarch Philip, brother of John the Baptist's enemy Herod Antipas, and named in honour of Caesar Augustus, the first Roman Emperor. It was there, in that Greek city with the Roman name, that Jesus was first openly acknowledged as the messiah of Hebrew expectation.

Rumours had been circulating that he must be Elijah, or another of the great prophets of the past, or John the Baptist come back from the dead. He questioned the disciples, 'But who do you say that I am?' and Peter replied 'You are the Christ.' Peter had recognized God's love and power in all that Jesus was and did. Matthew's account says that this was no ordinary 'flesh and blood' knowledge but spiritual insight.

Jesus knew that on such 'rock' (a play on words; rock in Greek is *petra*) one could build firmly, and he promised Peter 'the keys of the kingdom of heaven' – the right to exercise his authority on earth (Matt. 16.17-19). Was this authority different from that already given to the twelve?[2] Did Matthew single Peter out here because he wanted to put on record that Peter's later prominent position in the church was according to the Lord's will?

Whatever the answer to these questions, at that time Peter's perception was still only partial. When Jesus began to warn them

[2] Mark 6.7; Matt. 10.1; Luke 9.1. In Matt. 18.18 the words of 16.19 ('... whatever you bind on earth shall be bound in heaven, and whatever you loose on earth shall be loosed in heaven') are addressed to all the disciples.
Amongst the rabbis, 'to bind' was to declare an action unlawful, and 'to loose' was to declare it lawful.

that suffering and death lay ahead in Jerusalem,[3] Peter protested so vehemently that Jesus must have been reminded of the long struggle with temptation at the time of his baptism (cf. Matt. 16.23 and 4.10). Caesarea Philippi is often called the turning-point of the gospels. Peter's 'You are the Christ' was the climax of the forgiving, healing, befriending and teaching in Galilee and the neighbouring areas. From now on, Jesus must prepare the disciples for his death. God himself was to provide the climax of that – the resurrection, sign of the new life which Jesus' life of integrity had made available for all mankind.

The episode at Caesarea Philippi is a good illustration of Peter's character as we see it in the synoptic gospels. On the one hand, he has an intuitive perception which enables him to see Jesus with the eyes of faith, and the ability to commit himself to what he saw. On the other hand, his reactions are frequently impetuous and contradict his belief – like most men's. The thought of death, in particular, seems to provoke a violent reaction.[4]

Jesus had once warned the twelve of the costliness of discipleship;[5] now he called the crowds as well. What he had to say was true for all. A man must lose all selfishness, and face the difficulties life brings without opting out, in order to 'find' his real self – the man he has it in himself to become – and so 'save' his life. 'For whoever would save his life will lose it; and whoever loses his life for my sake and the gospel's will save it.'

3. Transfiguration
Mark 9.2-13 Matt. 17.1-13; Luke 9.28-36

Six days later something happened which revealed to Peter, James and John the reality of Jesus' relationship with God. He was transfigured before them so that they saw the glory which was normally

[3] Three times he predicted his rejection by the elders and chief priests (Mark 8.31; 9.31; 10.33-4).
[4] Luke 5.8. and Mark 9.5-6 reveal Peter's awe as he recognizes Jesus' holiness; and Matt 14.28-33 his trust in Jesus' power to keep him safe (yet even then his faith wavered and he lost his nerve). Mark 14.29,31, and Luke 22.33 are evidence of his commitment to Jesus; and yet he slept when Jesus had need of his support (Mark 14.37), and denied even knowing him when he was frightened of being arrested himself (Mark 14.66-72).
[5] See chapter 7.4.

veiled. Moses and Elijah appeared in the vision as if to witness that he was the one of whom the law and the prophets of the Hebrew scriptures had spoken.

Peter's reaction was to stay in that moment of vision, perhaps to return to the simplicity of Israel's time in the wilderness.[6] Then a voice spoke out of the cloud overshadowing the mountain on which they stood: 'This is my beloved son; listen to him.' Jesus was not merely the fulfilment of the law and the prophets of the old covenant and the Christ for whom Moses and Elijah had been a preparation, he was the beloved Son who spoke the words of God, and revealed his glory to the men of the new covenant.

On the way down the mountain they were puzzled because it had always been thought that Elijah would return before the messiah came. Jesus explained that John the Baptist had fulfilled Elijah's role. He urged them to keep secret what they had seen 'until the Son of man should have risen from the dead'. They did not understand what he meant; when it happened, the resurrection was totally unexpected.

4. The Epileptic Boy

Mark 9.14-29; Matt. 17.14-21; Luke 9.37-43

When he was once more among the crowds Jesus was asked to heal a boy who had convulsive fits in which he foamed at the mouth and became rigid so that he was in danger of rolling into water or fire.

This story is important for the father's honesty; he knew his faith was weak but trusted that Jesus could still help him (Mark 9.23-4): and for the source of Jesus' power to help (Mark 9.28-9; cf. Matt. 17.19-20). Through prayer God's power becomes active in a human situation. Prayer is a way to the kind of 'seeing' which leads to 'believing'.

---

[6] One of the annual feasts of Judaism, the Feast of Booths (or Tabernacles, as it was sometimes called), recalled the period when their ancestors lived in 'booths', shelters made of boughs and leaves, before their entry into Canaan. It was then that Yahweh had first revealed himself to his chosen people. Subsequent generations looked back to this as a period of purer worship. All this may have run through Peter's dazzled mind.

5. Eight Lessons in Discipleship

As they continued on the way, Jesus spoke of the responsibilities of life in the kingdom.

(i) They had already seen that closeness to God entails concern for others, and that prayer brings the power to help.

(ii) The next lesson was that true greatness lies in service of others (Mark 9.30-37; Matt. 18.1-5; Luke 9.46-8).

(iii) Followers of Christ are to be generous in recognizing the good deeds of others 'for he that is not against us is for us' (Mark 9.38-41; Luke 9.49-50).

(iv) Some self-discipline and self-denial is necessary so that the whole person is not stunted or maimed by over-indulgence of one part. If the 'salt' loses its saltness what is there to season it? (cf. Matt. 13.33; Mark 9.42-50; Matt. 18.6-9; Luke 17.1-2; 14.34-5).

(v) Marriage brings responsibility for one's partner which cannot be lightly thrown off, because in marriage the two become one (Mark 10.1-12). In Matthew 19.1-12 we have Jesus' reply when the disciples objected that this teaching against divorce was too difficult. He spoke of the call to celibacy 'for the sake of the kingdom of heaven' for those able to accept it.

(vi) A child-like trust and eagerness to receive what is offered is necessary for entry into the kingdom (Mark 10.13-16; Matt. 19.13-15; Luke 18.15-17).

(vii) A rich young man asked what he must do to gain eternal life. He wanted a deeper commitment in his life, but was unable to accept the call to renounce his possessions. Jesus knew that there are riches of greater value than material possessions, and these he promised to Peter and those who left all to follow him in the kingdom of God (Mark 10.28-30). Verse 18 may be a challenge to see that anything done in response to Jesus' teaching is in reality a response to God (Mark 10.17-31; Matt. 19.16-30; Luke 18.18-30).

(viii) When James and John Zebedee asked for the places of honour at Jesus' right and left hand he said that those who followed him must be servants as he himself was (Mark 10.32-45; Matt. 20.17-28; Luke 22.24-7).

6. Blind Bartimaeus of Jericho

Mark 10.46-52; Matt. 20.29-34; Luke 18.35-43

Jericho was the last town on the road to Jerusalem and the journey was nearly over. Suddenly a blind beggar[7] began to shout 'Jesus, son of David, have mercy on me!' Although the crowd told him to be quiet he persisted until Jesus heard and asked what he wanted. He asked for sight. Jesus said, 'Go your way; your faith has made you well.' However, Bartimaeus did not go his own way but like the true disciple whose faith leads on to sight he followed Jesus on the way . . .

REVISION QUESTIONS

1. What is the importance of the incident at Caesarea Philippi? What actually happened?

2. Both Jesus' baptism and the transfiguration on the mountain reveal something about (a) Jesus himself, and (b) his mission. What?

3. Describe in detail the scene that greeted Jesus and Peter, James and John when they came down from the mountain. What can be learnt from this incident about faith and prayer?

4. Describe what happened at (a) Bethsaida, and (b) Jericho, when Jesus healed the blind men.

---

[7] In Matt. 9.27-31 there is a healing of two blind men with features in common with Bartimaeus'. Possibly the incidents at Bethsaida and Jericho have been confused into a report of two blind men being healed at the same time.

12 *The Last Stage: Jerusalem*

Mark 11.1—12.44;14.1-11 and
parallel passages

The journey from Galilee to Jerusalem was almost over. Jesus' ministry in Galilee had brought him into conflict with the Pharisees and scribes. How would he be received by the religious leaders of Jerusalem?

Jerusalem was the heart of the Jewish nation, and the temple was the heart of Jerusalem. The purpose of the ritual of the temple was to remind man that he was man, standing before God. But it was possible to use it as a barricade to keep God at a safe distance, just as a meticulous concern with keeping every detail of the law could prevent his entering into the more vital aspects of a man's life. Jesus' real offence was that he brought God too close for comfort. He called him Father, and asked others to make a personal response to a Father's love. The only adequate response to love is to love in return. Those who could not bear the cost of loving God because it meant loving their neighbour also, rejected Jesus. The only final way to reject anyone is to put him to death.

In Jerusalem the tension between Jesus and the Sanhedrin would be aggravated by the political situation. The high priest and the seventy eminent men who formed the Sanhedrin valued their authority over Jerusalem and would not stand for anything that might give Rome cause to take it from them. The Roman Empire was tolerant of the religious practices of its subjects provided the peace was kept.

The annual festivals that brought pilgrims flocking to Jerusalem were a worry to Sanhedrin and Roman governors alike. The city was overcrowded, and nationalist feeling was at its height. The governor came into residence in the praetorium at these times, and the garrison of soldiers in the Antonia Fortress overlooking the temple was alert for the first sign of a popular uprising. Nerves were taut and the increased vigilance strained them to breaking-point.

This was the situation when Jesus entered the city a few days before the Feast of the Passover.

1. Sunday

(a) The entry into Jerusalem (Mark 11.1-10; Matt. 21.1-9; Luke 19.28-38)

His small band approached by the Jericho-Jerusalem road. They had passed the villages of Bethphage and Bethany, and as they neared the Mount of Olives Jesus sent two disciples to fetch an ass on which he then rode the last two miles. Zechariah the prophet had spoken of the messiah as 'humble and riding on an ass', bringing peace and unity to the nation through his kingship over the whole earth.[1] But no one realized the significance of Jesus' action: he was not the messiah the nationalists looked for, a prince of the house of David who would drive out the hated Romans, but the Servant–Son of the kingdom of God.

(b) Prediction of the destruction of Jerusalem and the temple (Luke 19.39-44; Mark 13.1-4; Matt. 23.37—24.3; Luke 13.34-5; 21.5-7)

Jesus did nothing to restrain the crowd's welcome, even though it revealed their misunderstanding of his vocation, but he knew that such nationalistic fervour would lead one day to Roman reprisals and that his people would stand no chance against them. Jerusalem's days were numbered. As the city came into sight he wept over it (Luke 19.39-44).

Later that week he spoke of the destruction of the temple (Mark 13.1-4). His words came true in AD 70 when after four years of bitter warfare culminating in the horrors of a five months' siege, the Romans took the city, looted and destroyed the temple, and took captive many thousands of the people for slavery or the gladiatorial games.

[1] Zech. 9.9-10; 14.9.

2. Monday

(a) The cleansing of the temple (Mark 11.15-19; Matt. 21.12-13; Luke 19.45-8)

On the day following his arrival, that is, on the Monday of what was to prove the last week of his life, Jesus went from Bethany where he was staying to the temple and drove out the money-changers and those selling pigeons for the sacrifices. He justified his action with the words: 'Is it not written, "My house shall be called a house of prayer for all the nations"? But you have made it a den of robbers.'

The Sanhedrin would not allow Roman currency in the temple; pilgrims had to buy the special temple coinage before they could purchase the birds or animals they wished to offer in sacrifice. Caiaphas the high priest and others were reputed to have made a considerable commission on the exchange. The pigeon-selling was also lucrative; pilgrims had no choice but to buy from the official market because each animal had to be certified 'ritually perfect'. Prices were whatever the monopoly liked to ask. These were the reasons why Jesus said the temple had been turned into a den of robbers.

Since the trading took place in the Court of the Gentiles, the only area into which non-Jews were allowed under penalty of death, the din of animals and barter made prayer impossible. The Sadducees were pleased to have so effectively excluded the despised Gentiles even from the outer court traditionally allowed them.

Jesus wished to restore the Court of the Gentiles to its proper use at the same time as he put an end to the exploitation of pilgrims.

When the chief priests, scribes and elders heard what had happened they knew they must get rid of him; his action was a criticism of their administration of the temple. But they dared not act openly because the majority of the people were on his side and any disturbance in the city would bring out the Roman troops.

(b) The incident of the withered fig tree (Mark 11.11-14,20-25; Matt. 21.18-22)

It is most unlikely that Jesus cursed a tree for not bearing fruit out of season. What is probable is that he told a parable against the leaders who had abused their position of trust, likening them to a barren fig tree which withered and died away because it was useless to God's people. We do know of two other parables in which fig trees are used in illustration. One taught that God always gives ample opportunity for repentance (Luke 13.6-9) and the other speaks of the inevitability of judgment (Mark 13.28-9). Attached to the parable, as we shall take it to be, of the withered fig tree are three sayings on faith, faith which the members of the Sanhedrin had failed to keep central in their lives:

(i) the necessity for faith in God's activity in human life;
(ii) faith in the power of prayer to influence all circumstances in life: '... whatever you ask in prayer, believe that you receive it, and you will'; and
(iii) the need for forgiving hearts before we pray, so that God can forgive us.

3. Tuesday

(a) The question of authority (Mark 11.27-33; Matt. 21.23-7; Luke 20.1-8)
The question of authority was a crucial issue in these last days in Jerusalem. The chief priests, scribes and elders had inherited position as members of the prominent priestly families and they had been educated in the rabbinic schools. On what grounds did a provincial carpenter, without formal theological training, presume to challenge it?

This was the first of a series of questions put by representatives of the different power groups within Judaism to try to trap the carpenter of Nazareth. Implicit in Jesus' counter-question is the belief that although neither he nor John had any man-given status they did have an authority of a higher kind.

The Christian church could only have come into existence because there was a wide-spread conviction that Jesus of Nazareth did reveal the will of God.

(b) The parable of the wicked tenants of the vineyard (Mark 12.1-12; Matt. 21.33-46; Luke 20.9-19)
Behind this parable lay the well-known song of the vineyard

(Isa. 5.1-7), in which Israel is depicted as the vineyard of the Lord, carefully prepared and planted with the choicest vines, protected and provided with everything needful, and yet yielding only useless wild grapes. It is more an allegory than parable, because 'the tenants' are the leaders of Israel who have consistently failed to produce 'fruit' worthy of their position of trust, despite the many warnings of the prophets down the centuries. In the parable/allegory the owner of the vineyard finally gives his vineyard to other tenants.

This parable is evidence that Jesus criticized the failure of the Sanhedrin to exercise a proper responsibility for God's people, and not the Jewish nation as a whole.

The chief priests and elders knew that it was told against them and they determined to arrest Jesus at the first possible moment. They could not do so while he was teaching openly in the temple for fear of provoking the crowd to retaliatory action.

Later, the Christian church thought of itself as the new tenant of God's vineyard, his new Israel.

(c) The question of tribute to Caesar (Mark 12.13-17; Matt. 22.15-22; Luke 20.20-26)

A mutual desire to get rid of the troublesome Nazarene had made allies of the Pharisees and Herodians in Galilee.[2] Now in Jerusalem they collaborated in putting the second trap question: was it lawful for a Jew to pay taxes to Caesar? If he answered yes, he would alienate those who, like the Pharisees and (for different reasons) the Zealots, maintained that Israel owed no allegiance other than to God. If he said no, he could be denounced to the Romans. He avoided either alternative. His answer was a further challenge to his opponents to see that true religion involved not just attendance at ceremonies and attention to rules, but a personal self-giving and commitment. They owed the state support for what it provided, but they owed themselves to God.

(d) The question concerning the resurrection (Mark 12.18-27; Matt. 22.23-33; Luke 20.27-40)

The Sadducees tried to entangle Jesus with a hypothetical in-

---

[2] Mark 3.6. See chapter 6.3(e).

stance of a woman who married seven brothers, one after the other as each husband died; whose wife would she be at the resurrection? Jesus refused to become involved in this specious and meaningless argument, and quoted from the scriptures which they claimed to accept.[3] The firm conviction of the new Israel was that they were the people of the living God who was active in the evolutionary creation-process, in human history, and in men's personal lives.

(e) The question of the greatest commandment (Mark 12.28-34; Matt. 22.34-40; Luke 10.25-8)

In answer to the scribe's question, Jesus combined two passages from the scriptures[4] to form a commandment of love for his new Israel. After this no one dared ask him any more such questions.

(f) Condemnation of hypocrisy (Mark 12.37-40; Matt. 23.1-36; Luke 11.39-52; 20.45-7)

Towards the end of this day of questions Jesus exposed the hypocrisies of those who liked to be thought pious and deserving of special respect, and yet neglected justice and mercy and faith (Matt. 23.23). Those who exalted themselves would be humbled (23.12). In time such honesty, seeing oneself as one really is (humility), became an ideal for all who followed the Christ.

(g) The widow's gift (Mark 12.41-4; Luke 21.1-4)

Before they left the temple that night he contrasted those who made a parade of their good deeds and a poor widow who put her two coins quietly in the offerings box. In the future Christian community, generosity was to be related to the cost to the giver, not the size of the gift.

4. Wednesday

The anointing at Bethany (Mark 14.1-9; Matt. 26.1-13)

Two days before the Feast of the Passover the chief priests and elders were still seeking a way to arrest Jesus without precipitating a public protest. In this tense and dangerous situation a woman

[3] Ex. 3.6.
[4] Deut. 6.5, the schema prayer which all Jews said daily, and Lev. 19.18.

showed him the highest honour a daughter of Israel could. Was this 'anointing' her acknowledgment that his authority came from God?

Some of those present thought that the ointment should have been sold (it was worth about £25 of our money), but Jesus said that there was plenty of opportunity to help the poor – if they really wanted to – and that the woman was, as it were, preparing his body for burial.[5]

5. Thursday

(a) The betrayal by Judas (Mark 14.10-11; Matt. 26.14-16; Luke 22.3-6)

The anointing incident at Bethany seems to have decided Judas Iscariot to betray Jesus. Matthew says he was given thirty pieces of silver. At one time in Israel this had been the price of a slave, and Zechariah once spoke of thirty shekels of silver as the wages of one he called 'the shepherd of the sheep doomed to be slain for those who trafficked in the sheep'.[6] The relevance of these two passages to the Servant–Son who would 'give his life as a ransom for many' (Mark 10.45) may have given rise to the tradition that Judas was paid thirty pieces of silver.

What was it that the chief priests paid Judas for? Was it for information? They certainly wanted to know where they could arrest Jesus away from the crowds, but they could easily have had him tailed. Perhaps they needed the witness of one of his own men that he did in fact claim to be messiah, in order to bring a charge of blasphemy for which the penalty under their law was death.

Why did Judas betray Jesus? There was a tradition that Judas was a thief and did it for the money, but surely Jesus would have known if he were a thief and have done something to help him before this. Was Judas taking revenge for his own disappointment that Jesus would not fulfil the role of warrior-deliverer? Or did he think he might force Jesus to rally Zealot support to save himself?

[5] There was a saying in the Hebrew scriptures that 'the poor will never cease out of the land.... You shall open wide your hand to your brother, to the needy and to the poor, in the land' (Deut. 15.11).
[6] Ex. 21.32 and Zech. 11.12.

74

(b) The death of Judas (Matt. 27.3-10)

Matthew alone reports Judas' suicide. When the priests would take no notice of his confession that he had betrayed an innocent man, Judas threw down the money they had given him and went out and hanged himself. The blood-money was later used to buy a burial-ground for foreigners.

Jesus forgave Peter, and would have forgiven Judas just as he had always forgiven anyone who repented. Perhaps Judas could not face himself after what he had done, but such shame is not the same as repentance. To ask forgiveness is to admit one's fault and to say 'I'm sorry'.

REVISION QUESTIONS

1. Describe Jesus' entry into Jerusalem. What two differing ideas about the messiah can be discerned in what was done and said?

2. What were Jesus' reasons for the cleansing of the temple?

3. Describe the anointing at Bethany as if you were an eyewitness. What significance did you, of Hebrew descent, see in the woman's action?

4. Discuss the possible motives of (a) the chief priests, and (b) Judas, for the monetary transaction mentioned in connection with Jesus' betrayal.

5. Summarize Jesus' teaching on the Tuesday of the last week of his life.

13 The End – and a New Beginning

Mark 14.12—15.20 and parallel passages

The Feast of the Passover commemorated the escape of the Hebrew tribes from slavery in Egypt.[1] Their descendants looked back on this event as a sign of God's concern for them, and kept 'the sacrifice of the Lord's passover' as one of the three great annual festivals of Judaism. A lamb for each household was sacrificed in the temple, and cooked and eaten within the family circle. It was very much a family commemoration in which the offering of life to God, the re-calling (remembering), of his 'saving acts' throughout history, and the covenant communion meal were made present realities in the life of his people.

Jesus had arranged to eat the passover supper with his 'family' of twelve in the upper room of a friend's house. The secrecy surrounding the preparation for the meal was a necessary precaution against Jesus' arrest before he had accomplished what was still to be done (Mark 14.12-16; Matt. 26.17-19; Luke 22.7-13).

1. The Last Supper – Communion Meal of the New Covenant

Mark 14.17-25; Matt. 26.20-29; Luke 22.14-23

When evening came Jesus and the twelve assembled in the upper room. Matthew says that Jesus let Judas know that he was going

---

[1] Ex. 22.21-8 is the earliest mention of the Passover in the Hebrew scriptures, and its connection with the exodus is explained. Ex. 24.7-11 describes the sealing of the covenant with Yahweh by means of the blood of the sacrificial animals, and the covenant 'communion' meal which followed. In Lev. 1.4-5 there is a description of the much later rite of the day of atonement for the cleansing of all Israel from sin.

to betray him. As they were eating, Jesus took the bread and after blessing and breaking it he gave it to them with the words: 'Take, eat; this is my body.' He blessed the wine and gave it to them saying: 'Drink of it, all of you; for this is my blood of the covenant, which is poured out for many for the forgiveness of sins' (Matt. 26.27-8).

Strange words at a familiar meal! We know that Jesus wanted his followers to remember all that had happened that last night: St Paul wrote to the people of Corinth that Jesus had said, 'Do this in remembrance of me.'[2] When they did so, they found that the risen Lord Jesus was still present with them in the breaking of bread, and this service became the covenant meal of the new Israel, the Lord's Supper. The full significance of his words was only gradually realized as they met together week by week, on the day of the resurrection, the 'first day of the week', our Sunday, to remember and to do what he had done on the night before he died.

In this act of worship they were able to unite the offering of their own lives with Jesus' self-giving life. The first Christians believed that they had been baptized not only into his death (which they believed was a victory over sin and evil), but also into the new quality of life which he had made a possibility for all men.

Through the breaking of bread they could recall, and so make real in the present moment, what they had come to see as the greatest of God's saving acts: his giving of himself to the world in and through the life of Jesus Christ.

By sharing in the meal of the new covenant made possible through Jesus' blood, that is, his offering of his life, they found that they had communion with the risen Lord and, through him, with God; he was the means by which a living relationship – communion – could now be established between God and men.

Jesus was accused at his trial of saying that he would destroy the temple and in three days raise it again. Obviously he was not speak-

---

[2] I Cor. 11.23-6. This letter contains the earliest record of the Lord's Supper that we have. It was written in the 50s of the first century, but Paul is reminding the Corinthian Christians of something they had long since known, '... what I also delivered to you', that is, what he had told them at some earlier date.

Other names by which the breaking of bread is known are the Lord's Supper, the Eucharist (from the Greek word for 'thanksgiving'), Holy Communion, Mass (from the Latin words at the end of the service when the people are *dismissed*, or *sent out*, to do the Lord's work in the world; these words are *ita, missa est* (from mittere=to send)).

ing literally: the temple had been forty-six years in building and was not even then completed. What did he mean? It was in the temple that the offering of the sacrificial animals took place. But an animal's life could not take the place of man's own self-giving, nor its blood make up for human sin. Only a human life of self-giving love could somehow 'absorb' the consequences of human evil. Jesus had accepted all that envy and fear and hatred could do to a fellow human being, and the resurrection proved him victor over it. After his death and resurrection his followers could see no further reason for animal sacrifice. His 'blood poured out for many for the forgiveness of sins' had taken its place. He had 'destroyed' the purpose for which the temple had been built.

2. The Garden of Gethsemane – Voluntary Acceptance of Death

Mark 14.26-42; Matt. 26.30-46; Luke 22.39-46

When the supper was over they went out to the Mount of Olives. On the way, thinking of his arrest which he knew might come at any moment, Jesus said that the twelve would run away and leave him. Peter swore that he would not, whatever others did. He was ready to go to prison and death rather than deny Jesus (Luke 22.33). But Jesus said that Peter would deny even knowing him.[3]

Finally they sat down in a garden, called Gethsemane. Jesus asked his three intimate friends[4] to watch with him while he prayed, but they fell asleep. His agonized prayer was the final battle with his natural shrinking from suffering and death; Luke tells us that it was so intense that his sweat was like drops of blood. But at the end of it he had found strength and waited calmly while Judas and the temple guards approached to arrest him. The humanity of Jesus is apparent in his fear of what lay ahead, and in his need for human companionship as well as prayer as he faced death. Death

[3] Mark 14.29-31; Luke 22.33-4. See also Mark 14.38. Jesus was right, however (Mark 14.50; Matt. 26.56). Peter's denial is in Mark 14.66-72; Matt. 26.69-75; Luke 22.56-62.
[4] Peter, James and John had been among the first of his disciples. They were the only ones he allowed in the room when he healed Jairus' daughter. They alone had the vision of his transfiguration. They are mentioned by name as being present at the healing of Simon Peter's mother-in-law (Mark 1.16-20; 5.37; 9.2; 1.29-31).

was no easier for him to accept than for any human being.

3. The Arrest – the Disciples' Desertion
Mark 14.43-52; Matt. 26.47-56; Luke 22.47-53

Judas identified the man they were to arrest by kissing him. Jesus prevented his followers from resisting, and asked why it had been necessary to arrest him in secret. He thus put his finger on the weakness of the chief priests' position: they loudly proclaimed their authority but in reality had not the support of the people. Jesus' friends ran away, one young man twisting out of his clothes to escape naked.

Later men wondered that God had not rescued Jesus. Matthew asserts that he could have called on 'twelve legions of angels'. The old temptation to help himself by supernatural means had to be faced even at this late hour, but he still refused to yield to it. He had given himself generously all his life; now he would accept death voluntarily rather than lose his real self by trying to save his life.[5]

4. Before the Sanhedrin
Mark 14.53—15.1; Matt. 26.57—27.2; Luke 22.54—23.1

(a) The final rejection

The Sanhedrin was assembled at the house of Caiaphas the high priest for an urgent night-time examination of the prisoner. Witnesses came forward but no two could be found whose evidence agreed, as was necessary under Jewish law before a man could be convicted.[6] Finally the high priest asked outright if he were 'the Christ, the Son of the Blessed?' Jesus' reply either consciously or unconsciously echoed the name by which Israel's God had made himself known to Moses,[7] and was interpreted as blasphemy. The high priest tore his robe in the traditional gesture that guilt had

---

[5] Mark 8.35. See chapter 7.4.
[6] Deut. 19.15.
[7] Ex. 3.13-15. The imagery in the words which follow 'I am' suggest that Ps. 110 and Dan. 7.13 were in his mind at this time. Ps. 110 may have been used at the enthronement of the kings of Judah. Daniel's vision is of 'a son of man' being given dominion over an everlasting kingdom.

been established and turned to the Sanhedrin. Their verdict was unanimous. They had rejected Jesus' teaching; now they rejected the man.

Since a trial held at night had no legal status the Council met again briefly as soon as it was morning, and then formally handed Jesus over to the Roman governor whose authorization was needed for any execution.

(b) Peter's denial

During the hearing at the high priest's house Peter had crept into the courtyard. He was frightened because it was not healthy to be known as the companion of an accused man. However, one of the maid's recognized him and bystanders noticed his Galilean accent. Peter lost his nerve and swore that he did not know the prisoner. When the crowing of the cock reminded him that Jesus had foretold this, he broke down and wept.

5. The Trial Before the Roman Governor
Mark 15.2-20; Matt. 27.11-31; Luke 23.2-25

(a) Pilate's question

Pontius Pilate was governor of Judea from AD 26 to AD 36. At the time Jesus was brought before him he had already made two blunders in handling 'incidents' in Jerusalem and knew that another mistake might end his career. The gospels portray Pilate as a man trying to evade responsibility for the trial, first by sending the prisoner to Herod Antipas (who merely sent him back without hearing any evidence);[8] and then by stating his own belief in Jesus' innocence.

The Roman governor's first question was 'Are you the king of the Jews?' Jesus answered 'You have said so.' He had not made this claim for himself but, as with the high priest's question, would not deny the truth when it was put by others. There is a notable differ-

[8] Luke tells us of this (23.6-16). As a Galilean Jesus came under the jurisdiction of Herod Antipas. The tetrarch's only interest in him was as a wonder-worker and when Jesus made no answer to his question Herod and his soldiers ill-treated him and returned him to Pilate. Herod and Pilate became friends after this. Indifference to the suffering they had in their power to inflict on an innocent man is the only obvious bond. Strange friendship!

ence between the high priest's and the governor's questions. Rome was not interested in the religious squabbles of a subject nation but a claim to kingship was treason against the Emperor.

(b) The charges

Luke states that there were three specific political charges. The prisoner, it was claimed, had been (a) perverting the nation; (b) telling the people not to pay taxes to Caesar; and (c) calling himself Christ a king. Each would have been sufficient ground for the death penalty if intention of rebellion against the Emperor could be proved.

The first charge may have had its origin in Jesus' challenge to the authority of Pharisees and Sanhedrin, and perhaps particularly in his clearing the Court of the Gentiles of the money and animal markets which the Sanhedrin had established.

The second may derive from his answer to the question about payment of taxes to Caesar, or even from what lay behind the strange incident in Matthew 17.24-7.

The welcome from the pilgrims when Jesus entered Jerusalem would have given substance to the third, and the high priest may well have twisted Jesus' answer to his question 'Are you the Christ, the Son of the Blessed' into a political accusation, 'He called himself Christ a king.' To the Romans the title 'Christ' did seem a rallying-call to Jewish patriots and revolutionaries.

Jesus made no answer to the three charges brought against him.

(c) Perversion of justice

Pilate could see that it was the envy of the leaders that had brought this prisoner before him. He tried to release him as a goodwill gesture. To release a popular prisoner at the Passover was a shrewd move to win the favour of the crowds towards the Roman administration. However, the priests began to stir up the mob to ask for Barabbas, a rebel and consequently a popular hero.

Pontius Pilate was the representative of Roman justice in Judea. He did not believe that the man before his court was guilty of treason and was reasonably sure that jealousy lay at the root of the trouble. Luke reports that Pilate declared three times 'I find no crime in this man' and, when the crowd clamoured 'Crucify him', demanded 'Why, what evil has he done?'[9] Yet when he feared that there might be a riot he washed his hands of responsibility, 'I am innocent of this man's blood', and handed him over for scourging and crucifixion. It is Matthew who tells us of the public hand-washing, and also of a dream which made Pilate's wife warn him to 'have nothing to do with that righteous man'.[10]

It may be that the evangelists wanted to whitewash Pilate by putting the responsibility for Jesus' death on the Jews. They would not wish to antagonize Roman officialdom and risk reprisals against other Christians in the difficult years of the last third of the first century when there was already sporadic persecution of Christians. Also, we know that Luke wanted to commend Christianity to the wider world outside Palestine; he would therefore want to show that its founder had been declared innocent in a Roman court of any political or criminal activity. Mark, writing his gospel in Rome, would not want to appear critical or resentful of Roman justice.

We have already noted the later bitterness towards the leaders of Judaism and it is possible that this is reflected in the reports we have of the trial of Jesus, especially of Matthew's.

This is not to say that the evangelists deliberately distorted the truth. But it is almost inevitable that their special interests and concern would make certain features of the trial stand out, and consequently take on greater significance in their reports.

Luke, however, said in his preface that he was writing an orderly account so that Theophilus might know the truth 'concerning the things of which you have been informed'; perhaps, Luke thought, in a biased manner which it was his job to correct.

(d) The game of king

When Pilate delivered Jesus up to be crucified, the soldiers took him into their barracks to play the popular game of 'King'. He was dressed in the Emperor's purple, given a reed for sceptre and a crown made of thorns, and then the soldiers knelt before him in mock homage.

Jesus the Nazarene was judged guilty of blasphemy by the Jewish Council, brought before a Roman court as a political offender and, although declared innocent by both the tetrarch of Judea and

[9] Luke 23.4,14,22.
[10] Matt. 27.24 and 27.19.

the Roman governor was, at the instigation of a Jerusalem mob, sentenced to execution as a criminal. The soldiers' mockery is perhaps nearest the truth: 'Hail, king of the Jews.'

(e) Whose responsibility?

The whole affair of Jesus' arrest and trial reveals much of the worst side of human nature. The Sanhedrin's deliberations show the lengths to which men will go to get rid of someone whose attitude to life seems a threat to their own. Peter's denial is a poignant example of how easily we lie to protect ourselves. Pilate demonstrates how justice can miscarry when a judge's first concern is for his own reputation. Most frightening of all, we see how mob violence ignores the rights of the individual.

It is impossible to attribute blame for Jesus' death to any one person or group. He was the victim of human prejudice, fear, indifference, and evil, as so many other human beings have been through the centuries. His voluntary acceptance of the role of victim ('the Son of man came ... to give his life as a ransom for many') has inspired men and women in every generation since to fight against these weaknesses in themselves, and in human society generally.

REVISION QUESTIONS

1. What part did Peter play in Jesus' life from the time of Caesarea Philippi to the crucifixion?

2. Write a character sketch of Peter, using all the incidents in which he figures.

3. Describe either the cleansing of the temple or the Last Supper. What meaning lies behind the outward words and actions? Can you see any relationship between the two incidents?

4. Read the account of the Last Supper (Mark 14.22-5) and the earliest account we have of the Christian eucharist (1 Cor. 11.23-6). What similarities are there?

5. Write brief notes on the parts played by the following in the last week of Jesus' life: (a) the woman at Bethany; (b) Judas; (c) Herod.

14 *Crucifixion and Resurrection*

Mark 15.21—end and parallel passages

Crucifixion was the method of execution reserved in the Roman Empire for slaves and criminals. The condemned man was fastened to the cross-bar and forced to walk through the streets to the place of execution where the uprights of the crosses stood permanently. He was stripped of his clothing, and tied or nailed to the cross-bar which was then hauled into position on the upright. Death came slowly, through exposure and exhaustion. It was a brutal form of execution and probably used to deter others from a similar crime, as the crucified man's offence was written up for all to see and his body left hanging until the cross was wanted for another unfortunate.

1. Crucifixion

Mark 15.21-32; Matt. 27.32-44; Luke 23.26-43

(a) Simon of Cyrene

Simon of Cyrene is the first to be mentioned of those who played a part in the crucifixion. He was compelled by the soldiers to help Jesus carry the heavy cross-bar to Golgotha, the skull-shaped hill outside Jerusalem where crucifixions took place. Simon Peter had sworn that he would not desert Jesus, but it was left to this other Simon to accompany Jesus to the end.

(b) The women of Jerusalem

Some women wept as Jesus passed them, but he told them to weep for themselves and their children. He knew the suffering that would fall on Jerusalem when Rome unleashed its full fury against the nationalist rebels (Luke 23.27-31).

(c) The soldiers

When they reached Golgotha Jesus was offered wine drugged with myrrh to deaden the pain, but he refused it. As they fixed his body to the cross at the third hour (9 a.m.) he said, 'Father, forgive them; for they know not what they do' (Luke 23.34). The inscription on the cross read: 'The King of the Jews'.

It was the custom for soldiers on duty at a crucifixion to take the condemned man's clothes; they cast lots to decide what each would have.

(d) The two thieves

Two thieves were crucified with him, taking the places James and John had asked for (Mark 10.35-45). One mocked Jesus, but the other turned to him as if repenting what had been wrong in his life (Luke 23.39-43).

(e) The bystanders' derision and mockery

The passers-by derided the helpless figure. Even the chief priests and scribes mocked, 'He saved others; he cannot save himself', and taunted him that they would believe he was the Christ if he came down from the cross; but it was because he voluntarily accepted death, that men came to believe in God's love for them (Mark 15.29-32).

2. Death

Mark 15.33-9; Matt. 27.45-54; Luke 23.44-9

With the sixth hour, midday, came darkness. A sudden sandstorm, an eclipse, the darkness of men's hearts? At the end of a further three hours Jesus cried out: 'My God, my God, why hast thou forsaken me?' (Mark 15.34). On the cross Jesus knew the terrible loneliness of those who feel themselves rejected by everybody, even God. At the ninth hour, 3 p.m., with a final cry he died. Luke tells us his words, words of trust in the Father whose presence he no longer felt but still could trust: 'Father, into thy hands I commit my spirit' (Luke 23.46).

The curtain-wall which separated the inner sanctuary of the temple split in two. Only the high priest had been permitted to enter that mysterious room, and then only on the day of atonement to sprinkle the blood of the sacrifice for the sins of his people; now the wall of separation had been broken. Was it an earthquake, as Matthew suggests? Or was it the symbolic tearing down of all that had separated men from God? Now, through Christ's life and death, God could be known by all men as 'Father'.

Since his own friends had run away it was left to a Gentile, the Roman centurion in charge of the crucifixion party, to speak Jesus' epitaph: 'Truly this man was son of God!'

We cannot tell from the Greek whether he said '*a* son of God' (which might not necessarily mean more than 'a good and righteous man') or '*the* Son of God'. *Divii Filius*, son of the divine, was a title of the Roman Emperor; the Roman soldier may have been making his comment on the inscription on the cross: this man died like a real king. But to Mark the Gentile officer's words expressed the conviction which swept through the Roman Empire in the years following the resurrection: the good news that Jesus Christ stood in a unique relationship to God which was best expressed by calling him Son of God. This conviction underlies the whole gospel.

3. Burial

Mark 15.40-47; Matt. 27.55-61; Luke 23.50-56

Jesus had not been entirely deserted by his own people. Mary Magdalene had been at the cross with another Mary and Salome, and some women who had looked after the disciples on the journey from Galilee. A member of the Sanhedrin even came forward to ask Pilate's permission to take the body down and bury it in his own private tomb.

This permission was granted when Pilate ascertained that the 'king of the Jews' was already dead. It must have taken courage for a man in Joseph's position to come forward openly declaring his interest in a criminal condemned by both Sanhedrin and Roman authority.

As the sabbath would begin at sunset (and no Jew could touch a dead body on the sabbath), there was little time for formalities. The body was hurriedly placed in a rock tomb, wrapped only in its linen shroud, and a heavy stone rolled across to seal the opening from animals. The two Marys were watching; they intended to return and embalm the body properly as soon as the sabbath was over. It was now Friday evening; they could return at dawn on Sunday.

4. The Empty Tomb

Mark 16.1-8; Matt. 27.62—28.8 and 11-15; Luke 24.1-12

The type of tomb in which Joseph of Arimathea laid Jesus' body was above ground, often a cave in the hillside in which narrow shelves were cut to receive the bodies. Later the bones were removed from the ledges to make way for another body and placed in an inner chamber. It is still possible, in modern Israel, to see the remains of these old tombs.

When the sabbath, the Saturday, was over the two Marys and Salome brought spices to prepare the body for permanent burial. It was sunrise on the first day of the new week, our Sunday. They had carefully noted the position of the tomb, but now wondered how they would roll back the stone at the entrance. Then they saw that the stone had been moved already and, on entering, met a young man, who said to them that Jesus of Nazareth had risen and would meet them in Galilee. The women fled from the tomb trembling. They said nothing to any one because they were afraid at what they could not understand.

This is Mark's account of the finding of the empty tomb. The other two are substantially the same. Matthew speaks of the man who gave the message as an angel, possibly because many Jews thought that the holy God only approached men through such intermediaries. Luke says that there were two men, and that the women *did* tell the apostles but they dismissed the story as 'an idle tale'. The message in Luke is also different from that in Mark. The women were reminded that, while they were still in Galilee, Jesus had spoken of his death and rising again. Since Luke seems to know only the tradition of Jesus' post-resurrection appearances in the neighbourhood of Jerusalem, it is unlikely that he would

87

have known of a message that Jesus would meet them in Galilee.

Most of the resurrection appearances of Jesus are in the neighbourhood of Jerusalem, though there was also a tradition that the disciples saw him in Galilee.

Matthew has an intriguing story of a guard at the tomb (27.62-6; 28.4,11-15). Probably a rumour had been circulating that Jesus' body had been stolen by the disciples and buried elsewhere, and Matthew wanted to make public the origin of the rumour. That it was without foundation is proved by the courage of the disciples; they could never have withstood persecution to establish the Christian church if they had known the empty tomb to be a hoax. Nor, of course, if his body had been buried secretly would anything have prevented that place from becoming a famous centre of pilgrimage.

5. Appearances of the Risen Lord

Mark 16.9-20; Matt. 28.9-10,16-20; Luke 24.13-53

(a) The appendix to the Gospel of Mark (16.9-20)

The RSV translation of the New Testament prints the Gospel of Mark as if it ended at verse 8. Verses 9-20 are printed in a footnote as an appendix to the gospel proper. These verses are not in all manuscripts, and the style is different from that in which the rest of the gospel is written; they were probably added later, though by the second century because Tatian and Irenaeus who wrote then know of them.

Did Mark intend to end on the dramatic note of verse 8, with the women running from the empty tomb? Or was he killed, perhaps in the Neronian persecution of Christians in the 60s of the first century, before he could write his final words? Or did he, like Matthew and Luke, report the appearances of the risen Lord to the disciples and the end of the papyrus scroll has been torn and lost? We shall probably never know the answer to these questions, but two attempts were made to supply the omission: the 'shorter ending', as it is called, is in only a few manuscripts; the 'longer ending' is that printed as an appendix to the Gospel according to Mark. It reports three appearances of Jesus after the resurrection, all in or near Jerusalem:

(i) to Mary Magdalene, who told others but they did not believe her;

(ii) to two unnamed men as they were walking in the country, who also told the apostles and were not believed;

(iii) to the eleven as they sat at table; Jesus scolded them for not having believed the others and told them to continue their mission throughout the world.

The church had of course been doing this for a generation or more (we do not know when the Markan appendix was written), and the language of the final verses reflects the experience of the first Christians.

(b) In the Gospel of Matthew (28.9-10 and 16-20)

Matthew records two appearances of the risen Jesus:

(i) to Mary Magdalene and the other Mary as they were running from the tomb; he repeated the message they had been given already, that Jesus would meet his disciples in Galilee;

(ii) to the eleven apostles *in Galilee*; there Jesus commissioned them to make disciples of all nations and to baptize and teach as he had taught them. (The mention of the Trinity, the Father, Son and Holy Spirit in the formula of baptism reflects the practice of the church in Matthew's own day; at first Christians were baptized in the name of the Lord Jesus only.)

(c) In the Gospel of Luke (Luke 24.13-53)

Luke reports five appearances, all of them in or near Jerusalem:

(i) to some unnamed women (vv.22-4);

(ii) to Cleopas and another man on the road to Emmaus, a village seven miles from Jerusalem, who did not at first recognize this stranger who explained how the scriptures spoke of the suffering and death of the Christ;

(iii) to Simon Peter (v.34);

(iv) to the eleven apostles and others with them just after the arrival of the two men from Emmaus, when he told them to be his witnesses after they had received 'power from on high';

(v) to a large company, at Bethany, where he blessed them and then left them.

The note of joy on which Luke ends his gospel is the essential message of the resurrection of Jesus. God's power, which had filled his earthly life, was henceforth available to all men and women to help them find meaning and purpose in their own lives.

(d) Other documentary evidence

There is further evidence of resurrection appearances of the risen Lord Jesus in the Gospel according to John and in Paul's first letter to the Corinthians (15.3f.). Although differing in details, as we have seen the synoptic gospels themselves do, the following facts are confirmed by this further documentary evidence: the tomb in which the dead body of the crucified man was placed on Friday afternoon was empty on Sunday morning; Jesus was seen, though he was 'different' and not immediately recognizable, by individuals and by groups of people in and near Jerusalem and, according to one tradition, also in Galilee; the resurrection was completely unexpected.[1] This fact, that the resurrection was not expected, means that the disciples could not have imagined they 'saw' Jesus out of wishful thinking. The very possibility of resurrection was as incredible to them as it is to us – until their own experience convinced them.

(e) The church and Christian experience as evidence

But the most compelling evidence for the resurrection of Jesus Christ is the existence of the Christian church. Unless his followers believed that he had triumphed over sin and death they would have remained in hiding, disappointed and frightened men, until they were able to get out of Jerusalem safely and back to their fishing nets. Only their trust that God was at work, that God had at last intervened in the greatest of his 'saving acts', accounts for their new courage and the super-human resources with which they 'conquered' the Roman Empire for Christ.

Christianity could have continued to attract converts and to spread only because other men and women found that Christ's

---

[1] See Mark 9.10, where the disciples are puzzled by the expression 'rising from the dead'. The actual language in which Jesus' predictions of his death are reported have been coloured by the evangelists' knowledge of what actually did happen. The disciples' fear and despondency (e.g. Luke 24.17-24) show that Jesus' death had put an end to their hopes.

life was living in them: they were 'in Christ' and could not deny the reality of their own experience.

No one would have thought of writing a gospel unless he had experienced in his own life the power of Jesus' victory and known it to be, in truth, 'good news'.

Further (although it is a relatively minor point), there is no conceivable reason for the switch from the sabbath (Saturday) to the first day of the week (Sunday) as the day of worship unless something had happened to show decisively that the old order was ended, and new life for the new Israel had begun.

NOTE ON CHRISTIAN BELIEF IN THE RESURRECTION

Belief in the resurrection of the dead does not mean that Christians think that the dead are resuscitated (brought back to life), or that the decomposed particles of dead bodies are somehow reconstituted. Rather does it express the conviction that what is of real and lasting (eternal) value could not come to a final end, and that in some at present unknown mode the persons we have become in this life, the *real* person, not the outward appearance, will continue to be, without the limitations of, or need for, a material body occupying space and time. The manner of its happening no one knows. It can only be accepted in faith.

REVISION QUESTIONS

1. What was the attitude to Jesus displayed by (a) the two thieves; (b) the passers-by; (c) the chief priests and scribes; (d) the centurion; (e) the two Marys?

2. What were Jesus' words as reported in the synoptic gospels (a) when he was crucified; (b) to the repentant thief; (c) at the ninth hour; (d) immediately before he died? Give examples from the gospels to show how (a), (b), (d) seem to sum up his attitude to God and to men throughout his life. In what way is (c) like the temptation experience?

3. List the appearances of Jesus after the resurrection as reported

in each of the synoptic gospels. How might we account for the discrepancies?

4. Describe in detail the meeting on the road to Emmaus and all that happened subsequently that night.

5. Using any information in the synoptic gospels, reconstruct the events of the Sunday morning after the crucifixion.

15 *Mark Thirteen – the 'Little Apocalypse'*

Mark 13 and related passages
in Matt. 24 and Luke 21

We did not study the information in Mark 13 when we came to it because it is impossible to say what place it had in the actual ministry of Jesus. Mark 13 looks like a long speech by Jesus in answer to Peter, James and John's question: when would the destruction of the temple take place? But it is more likely that it is Mark's own compilation. In much the way that Matthew collected Jesus' teaching and presented it as if it were one sermon on a mountain, Mark has incorporated various sayings of Jesus about the future into a typically Jewish apocalyptic setting.

The word *apocalyptic* means 'revealed'. An *apocalypse* is something that purports to reveal the future by means of imagery and symbolism. Its purpose in Jewish literature was to give hope in desperate times. For example, when it was not safe to speak openly against the government during the centuries of foreign domination apocalypses were written whose symbolism was meaningful to those for whom they were intended, but the actual references were veiled to the outsider. The visions in the Book of Daniel gave Jews of the second century BC hope of ultimate survival in spite of their present suffering under the tyrant Antiochus III, although they seemed to refer to events of four hundred years earlier. It appeared to be history but was in fact an imaginative description of a future in which Antiochus Epiphanes had met his just deserts. Similarly, the purpose of the last book of the New Testament, the Revelation to John, was encouragement of Christians undergoing persecution towards the end of the first century AD, but all factual references to place and time are hidden under the symbolism of heavenly visions.

Before we can begin to understand what the apocalyptic passages in the synoptic gospels mean, we must know something of the political and social situation which gave rise to this, to us, strange and difficult literary medium.

The uneasy tension between the people of Palestine and their Roman rulers (the wars and rumours of wars of Mark 13.7) had led many to think that the end of the world was near. Christians expected Christ's return for the judgment 'at the end of the age'. This expectation, allied to the fear of the imminent end of the world, gave rise to rumours that he had actually been seen (13.21-2). To put an end to speculation which was disrupting everyday life Mark wrote that the Lord had warned of such a situation but had also said that 'the end is not yet' (13.6,7,23). Troubled times should make men look to the quality of their present lives and determine to live as men prepared to stand at any moment in God's presence, rather than lead them into escapism (13.33,35,37).

Luke is even more explicit about the effect the rumours and speculation was having on some people: '... take heed to yourselves lest your hearts be weighed down with dissipation and drunkenness and cares of this life, and that day come upon you suddenly like a snare ... watch at all times, praying that you may have the strength to escape all these things that will take place, and to stand before the Son of man' (21.34-6).

In this passage we see the two characteristics of synoptic apocalyptic: the references to actual historical events, and the 'outside-history' challenge which faces all human beings. Because these two are woven together the 'little apocalypse', as it is called, is very confusing.

The historical references are to the occasional persecutions of Christians during the last third of the first century, and to the devastation caused by the Jewish-Roman war of AD 66-70. Matthew and Luke were writing after that date; they knew the horrors of the siege and destruction of Jerusalem even if they had not been actually living there then. Mark was writing his gospel in the tense situation which led up to it, and quite possibly suffered himself during Nero's persecution of Christians living in Rome. It was inevitable that the evangelists' own experience would colour their reporting of any of Jesus' remarks about the future: they would think that he must have been referring to the events which were so catastrophic to them. Jesus could have foreseen the destruction of the Jewish nation, just as any man sensitive to the nationalism of his people and the inexorable might of Rome. But it is now impossible for us to know exactly what he said, and what the evangelists have added or altered because of their own knowledge of what actually happened.

The 'outside-history' challenge which Jesus put before men are the questions which all human beings have to answer: how we are to respond to the search for meaning and purpose and fulfilment, what is the meaning of existence, what is the relationship of God to the world and to each one of us individually? The little apocalypse of Mark 13 is – just that: an attempt to reveal the ultimate purpose of God for man, and to reassure readers of the 'in-time' triumph of the kingdom which Jesus, as the Christ, has established (13.26). We may say that the purpose and meaning of Mark 13 and similar passages in the synoptic gospels is the 'unveiling' of the end or goal of human existence so that we may understand how best to live in the present.

Mark has placed this warning/reassurance immediately before the passion narrative as a reminder that the betrayal, suffering, trial, crucifixion and death of Jesus happened not to a helpless victim of circumstance, but to the Son of man who gave his life in order that his Spirit might be freed for all men to share in it. His way of living was the victorious way, and he is able to help us live that way. We have a revelation through Jesus Christ of what it means to be a human being: the natural human life is lived in communion with God.

NOTE ON 'THE SECOND COMING'

For a while the first Christians expected Christ to return to earth during their lifetime, but quite soon they came to see that God's purpose had been fully revealed by the resurrection, and that Jesus Christ had already come to his people at Pentecost, and continued to be present with them in the breaking of bread. There was no need for a further coming of Christ because he had already accomplished the full purpose of the incarnation.

Nevertheless belief in a 'second coming' has persisted, and to this day some point to signs which they say herald it.

The New Testament witness as a whole suggests that the apocalyptic symbolism and imagery of the 'coming of the Son of man in clouds with power and glory' (13.26) is a way of saying that history finds its fulfilment and end beyond space and time. Even though the kingdom of God must be accepted and entered here and now, in historical time, its final fulfilment and completion is outside the narrow confines of this life.

PART TWO

16 *The Parables in Matthew and Luke*

Jesus' contemporaries spoke of him as a teacher, though so far as we know he was not, strictly speaking, a rabbi because he had not had a formal theological training in the rabbinic schools. He spoke with a personal authority, unlike the official teachers who merely passed on the opinions of rabbis of earlier generations.[1] The ordinary people flocked to hear him speak; Luke says they 'hung upon his words'.[2] Educated men, too, listened with respect. We are told twice that Herod wanted to see him.[3] When the learned men of Jerusalem tried to trap him he parried their questions skilfully, and his replies were a further challenge to their attitudes so that they gave up their attempt to make him convict himself out of his own mouth.[4]

Jesus taught in the synagogues,[5] and addressed the crowds thronging the temple courts at the great feasts.[6] He frequently spoke in the open air, on one occasion from a boat pushed out from the shore so that his voice could reach the large crowd.[7] We have a few reports of his advice to those who approached him as he travelled through the countryside,[8] but the greater part of the teaching which has come down to us in the gospels is instruction to disciples, in the form of parables.

[1] Mark 1.22.
[2] Luke 19.48.
[3] Luke 9.9; 23.8-9.
[4] Chapter 12(3).
[5] Mark 6.2; Luke 4.16-30; 13.10.
[6] Mark 11.15-18; 12.35ff.; 14.49.
[7] Mark 4.1.
[8] For example, the rich young man who wanted to know the way to eternal life, Mark 10.17-31; Matt. 19.16-30; Luke 18.18-30; (chapter 11.5(vii)).

The five parables of Mark 3.22—4.34 would have reassured the men of the kingdom of the ultimate success of the mission which they shared with Jesus. We shall now study the further parables in Matthew and Luke under four headings: parables of discipleship, parables of watchfulness, parables of God's love and compassion, parables of judgment. The parables on prayer and forgiveness are dealt with in chapter 19.

In many of the parables we have the words 'the kingdom of God' or, as Matthew prefers, 'the kingdom of heaven'; but even when the kingdom is not expressly mentioned or implied the parables are still offering guidance to the follower of Christ who wishes to accept the reign of God in his heart and life. To accept God as king is to enter the kingdom.

1. Parables of Discipleship

(a) Parable of the leaven (Matt. 13.33; Luke 13.20-21)

Just as leaven (yeast) makes dough rise, so the sons of the kingdom are to transform the society in which they live. The first Christians were once described as 'these men who have turned the world upside down' (Acts 17.6). The revolutionary transformation must first take place in the life of the disciple, then, through him, in the world.

(b) Parables of the hidden treasure and the pearl of great price (Matt. 13.44-6)

The kingdom is of infinite value and worth the renunciation of anything incompatible with membership. The note of joy in these parables puts the selling or renunciation in the right perspective. It is a giving up only in order to have what one values more.

(c) Parable of the talents (Matt. 25.14-30) and the parable of the pounds (Luke 19.11-27)

A master entrusted his property to his servants while he was away on a journey. He gave three men five, two and one talents respectively (a talent was a large sum of money worth, perhaps, £500 of our money). The first traded with his five talents and made five talents more, and the second man also doubled his original two talents. The man with the one talent hid it in the ground, either out of reluctance to take responsibility for putting it to good use or through laziness. The reward of the faithful servants was joy; the joy of their master.

Discipleship entails making full use of one's gifts and talents for the common good; it was not their own profit they were seeking. The parable's teaching holds good whether 'talent' is the money, or one's natural or acquired skills.

The parable of the pounds is similar. A nobleman entrusted one pound to each of ten servants. On his return home, the first servant to report had turned the pound into ten, and the second had turned his into five. The third man had hidden his pound, and it was taken from him and given to the servant with ten pounds.

The reward for the industry and enterprise of the two 'profitable servants' was increased responsibility.

(d) Parable of the unjust steward (Luke 16.1-13)

Jesus used the story of a dishonest steward who, under notice of dismissal, allowed his rich master's customers to halve the amount they owed so that they would look after him when he was out of a job, to teach the necessity for ingenuity and foresight as well as faithfulness. The 'sons of light' should be as enterprising in seeking the good of the kingdom as a man is in looking after his own self-interest. 'I tell you' in v.9 introduces Jesus' comments on the story. His teaching on faithfulness is:

(i) money should be used to build up values which are eternal ('unrighteous mammon' is a reference to money which can so easily be used for unjust (unrighteous) purposes);

(ii) faithfulness in little things must come before we can be trusted with 'the true riches';

(iii) no one can serve two masters with single-minded devotion; disciples must choose whether it is to be God they serve with love, or 'mammon'.

Probably the 'unjust steward' was a real person whom everyone was talking about: he had just been discovered faking the accounts. Jesus used him as an example to 'the sons of light': they should be as enterprising for the kingdom as a man looking after his own self-interest.

(e) Parable of the good Samaritan (Luke 10.25-37)

For this parable we are indebted to a lawyer's question: who is the neighbour we are to love? Jesus replied by telling the story of a man who was travelling the seventeen-mile long Jericho-Jerusalem road and was attacked, stripped and beaten, and left half-dead. This particular road was infested with bandits and it was dangerous to linger on it. A priest, and then a Levite, saw the man lying by the road and passed on hurriedly on the other side. Although he was not of the same race or religion, a Samaritan stopped and attended to the man's injuries as best he could, put him on his own animal, and took him to an inn to be cared for, paying something on the spot and promising to reimburse the innkeeper any further expense. It is a man's needs, and not his relationship to us, nor even his attitude or treatment of us, that determine our responsibility towards him.

2. Parables of Watchfulness

(a) Parable of the ten maidens (Matt. 25.1-13)

It is still the custom in modern Palestine for the bridegroom to come to the bride's house at night and, accompanied by the bridal procession, take her to his parents' house for the marriage ceremony. When the ceremony is over the marriage-feast begins. The lamps in the parable are really 'torches': rushes or tow soaked in oil and attached to the end of a pole. The oil had to be replenished at frequent intervals. Five of the bridesmaids had carelessly forgotten to bring flasks of oil. When their torches began to go out they had to go and buy more at the all-night bazaars in the market-place. By the time they reached the bridegroom's house the marriage was over and the feast had begun. They were excluded; the bridegroom said 'I do not know you' – there is no place for you.

In the east a wedding often symbolized salvation. The Hebrews expected God's reign on earth to begin with a messianic banquet, and the Pharisee's were confident that they, as Yahweh's 'chosen people', would be present at it. The parable of the ten maidens is a warning that salvation is not guaranteed; men have to be prepared at all times to recognize and accept God's invitations which come in and through the events of everyday life.

(b) Parable of the waiting servants (Luke 12.35-8)

In this the master is at a marriage-feast and his male servants are commended for being prepared, whatever the hour of his return.

(c) Parable of the thief at night (Luke 12.39-40; Matt. 24.43-4)

'You must also be ready; for the Son of man is coming at an hour when you do not expect.'

Here man's preparedness is shown by his response to the Son.

(d) Parable of the faithful and wise steward (Luke 12.41-6; Matt. 24.45-51)

Peter asked if the previous parables were just for them or for all (Luke 12.41). In reply Jesus compared 'the faithful and wise servant' who worked honestly in his master's absence with one who abused his position of trust to get drunk and ill-treat those under him. It is the person we are and what we do that counts, not the front we put on for others to see.

(e) Parables of the tower-builder and the king going to war (Luke 14.25-35)

These twin parables teach that discipleship is costly because any-thing incompatible with life in the kingdom must be renounced. Important decisions require that a man carefully assesses the whole situation, as a king does before he goes into battle. Is the joy and responsibility of the kingdom and fellowship with God what is desired above all else?

The parables of discipleship and watchfulness teach that one must consider carefully the 'riches' of life in the kingdom, count the cost, and make a single-minded commitment. Neighbourliness, re-sponsibility in the use of one's gifts, and faithfulness are expected of a disciple.

3. Parables of God's Love

(a) Parable of the lost sheep (Luke 15.1-7; Matt. 18.12-14)

When Pharisees and scribes objected to Jesus talking to and eating with tax collectors and sinners who came to listen to his teaching, he justified his attitude by telling three parables of God's compassion for 'the lost'.

This first parable would have appealed to countrymen. God's love goes out to seek and save the straying.

(b) Parable of the lost coin (Luke 15.8-10)

Palestinian women still today wear their marriage dowries in head-dresses of gold and silver coins. Besides being their main adornment, they are security against widowhood or misfortune. The woman in the parable was very poor; her ten silver drachma were worth perhaps £1.

(c) Parable of the lost son (prodigal son) (Luke 15.11-32)

The third parable of the lost is a story-parable, and unlike most parables has two points.

A younger son asked for his inheritance so that he could leave home and lead an independent life. He had a good time with his money, but when it was spent he found it difficult to get work because there was a famine in the country in which he found himself. Feeding pigs, which to a Jew were unclean, would be the lowest possible occupation for him to take. Desperation at last overcame the boy's pride and he went home to ask his father to take him back as a hired servant. However, his father reinstated him as a son of the house.

The elder son resented the welcome given to his no-good brother, even though his own position was not affected by it in any way. This second point was a challenge to the self-righteous Pharisees and scribes to see that although they begrudged salvation to those they called sinners, God's concern extended to all, whether 'lost' through their own fault, or through circumstances beyond their control.

These three parables of the lost would comfort those who had thought themselves outcast for ever because of some past sin. Again we hear the note of joy which is a characteristic of the kingdom Jesus introduced on earth.

(d) Parable of the labourers in the vineyard (Matt. 20.1-16)

In this parable the kingdom is likened to an employer who gave a day's pay to the men he employed, whether or not they had done a full day's work. It was not the men's fault that they could not get work, and each needed a day's pay to buy a day's food for his family. He paid according to need rather than earnings. Those who were 'late arrivals' were assured the same chance of salvation : repentant ex-sinners were not inferior to righteous Pharisees, nor Gentile Christians to Israel who expected a privileged position in God's kingdom.

(e) Parable of the barren fig tree (Luke 13.6-9)

On observing that a certain fig tree had borne no fruit for three years, the man in whose vineyard it stood ordered it to be cut down. His vinedresser offered to dig round it and manure it in the hope that it would bear fruit next year; if it still bore no fruit despite his extra care then he would cut it down.

God's love gives every chance for repentance and a new life that bears fruit. If these opportunities are refused, our 'barrenness' is our own fault.

These parables teach that God's love seeks out the lost and outcast, that it is concerned with each individual's need, and that it gives ample opportunity for all to respond to it with an answering love. The judgment which we bring on ourselves by refusing to accept love and to love in return is the subject of the following five parables.

4. Parables of Judgment

(a) Parable of the weeds (Matt. 13.24-30)

The kingdom is compared to a man who sowed good seed in his field, but during the night his enemy scattered weeds. As with the parable of the sower (Mark 4.1-9), an interpretation has been added in which the Son of man sows the good seed and 'the evil one' the weeds; the harvest is the judgment 'at the end of the age'.[9] Notice the 'apocalyptic' language similar to that of Mark 13 (see chapter 15).

This parable teaches the inevitability of judgment, but also warns against man's critical, premature judgments. We are not in

[9] The origin of the interpretations is discussed in chapter 8.2.

a position to judge our fellow-men and by doing so may harm what is of value in them: root up the wheat with the weeds. Judgment must be left to 'the harvest'.

(b) Parable of the fishing-net (Matt. 13.47-50)

Whereas the parable of the weeds would have been a suitable analogy of judgment for farmers, this would have more appeal to fishermen.

The kingdom is open to all; there is no discrimination between 'fish of every kind': men of all races, colours, temperaments, backgrounds are invited. Nevertheless there is a sorting out at the end of the age of those whose lives have rendered them either fit or unfit. Once more we see the typical imagery of Jewish apocalyptic, in 'the fire' and 'gnashing of teeth'.

(c) Parable of the marriage feast (Matt. 22.1-14) and the parable of the banquet (Luke 14.16-24)

The custom in the east was to send out an invitation a long way ahead and then to follow it up with a personal reminder immediately before the marriage.

In the parable the invited guests made excuses at the last minute: they were too busy for one reason or another. The king whose son's marriage was being celebrated was very angry at this discourtesy. He sent his servants into the streets to invite anyone, good and bad, so that the wedding-hall should still be filled with guests. Those first invited were not indispensable.

This parable was a grim warning that Israel's status as God's chosen did not guarantee salvation: each individual's personal response is necessary. The invitation into the kingdom had now gone out to all mankind. This is the 'universalism' in Jesus' teaching which annoyed the Pharisees.

Surely, however, it was unfair of the king to complain as he did of his guests' dress when he had invited them in off the streets? Yet when we remember that to Jesus' hearers the marriage-feast of a king's son would symbolize the messianic age which they hoped would bring universal salvation for all Israel, the significance of the wedding garment becomes clear. It is the forgiveness with which we must be clothed, the forgiveness which in a sense *is* salvation, and it is ours as soon as we repent. The man without the wedding garment was to blame; he had not asked for what was freely offered him.

Verse 7 is probably a reference to the destruction of Jerusalem in AD 70 when its inhabitants were killed and the city burnt by the Romans. Many in Matthew's day thought the fall of Jerusalem was a judgment on its unrepentant people.

Luke's parable of the banquet is similar, although its imagery is more suited to his Greek readers.

The second invitation is to 'the poor and maimed and blind and lame'. Luke has a great compassion for the outcast and inadequate. It was he who recorded Jesus' sermon in the synagogue at Nazareth at the outset of the Galilean ministry when Jesus quoted Isaiah's prophecy that in the day of messiah good news would be given to the poor and the blind, the prisoners and the oppressed (Luke 4.16-30). Now we see that Luke prefaced his version of the parable with Jesus' advice to those who were in a position to give banquets: '... when you give a feast, invite the poor, the maimed, the lame, the blind, and you will be blessed, because they cannot repay you ...' (Luke 14.12-15).

Since each one of us is in some way 'maimed' and inadequate to the stresses and problems life presents, and to some degree mentally or spiritually 'blind', we are reassured by this parable that our defects do not exclude us from the blessings of the kingdom. It is not what we have been endowed with by nature or given by a helpful environment, but our readiness and willingness to answer when called: to do what we can with what we have, that gives our lives real, or eternal, worth.

(d) Parable of the sheep and goats (Matt. 25.31-46)

The imagery in this parable is again that of Jewish apocalyptic: the angels, the judgment-throne, the judgment day at the end of the age, eternal punishment. Into this setting the figure of the Son of man is introduced as the one who occupies the place of judgment. The criterion by which each is judged is whether or not he has acted with compassion and mercy towards his fellow-men. Both 'sheep' and 'goats' are surprised at the verdict they receive, but the Son of man says: '... as you did it to one of the least of these my brethren, you did it to me.' The parable is thus teaching Jesus', and therefore God's, involvement with mankind.

Jesus was brought up in Judaism's severe doctrine of judgment. Nevertheless, in his actual dealings with men and women he did not judge. When he was face to face with a sinful woman he forgave her.[10] When he was asked to make a brother share an inheritance he said to the one who asked him: 'Man, who made me a judge over you?' and warned him of the danger of putting too great a value on material possessions.[11] When Martha complained that her sister Mary left her to do the housework while Mary listened to Jesus and sat at his feet,[12] he refused to do anything about the criticism and in fact chided Martha, and when he did speak of the inevitability of judgment he made it clear that it was our refusal to meet the needs of our brothers that judged us. His own reaction to personal injury is consistent with his teaching: when James and John wanted retribution because a Samaritan village would not give Jesus hospitality he rebuked them,[13] and even in the agony of crucifixion he would not judge his tormentors: 'Father, forgive them; for they know not what they do.'[14]

(e) Parable of the rich man and Lazarus (Luke 16.19-31)

In this story-parable judgment is pictured as separation from what, with a new awareness, is recognized as good. There is no intention of describing what happens after death: hell (or heaven) is not a place, and our condition after death cannot be pictured in physical terms. 'Abraham's bosom' suggest a place of honour for the beggar who was despised in this life.

The teaching is that the choices we make day by day have eternal significance. Our own actions and attitudes are making us into a certain kind of person, and no power from outside ourselves can alter the natural consequence of the life we have chosen to lead. All have some knowledge of good and understanding of mercy, the equivalent of Moses' and the prophets' teaching; if we choose to ignore it we destroy ourselves, as did the rich man in this parable.

---

[10] Luke 7.36-50; chapter 19.2(d).
[11] Luke 12.13-21, the story of the rich fool.
[12] Luke 10.38-42.
[13] Luke 9.51-6.
[14] Luke 23.34.

REVISION QUESTIONS

1. Tell the parable of the talents. In what ways does Luke's parable of the pounds differ?

2. What do the three parables of the lost reveal of God's concern for men? Recount any one in detail.

3. In commercial and industrial life payment is made only for work done. The parable of the labourers in the vineyard suggests that this may not always be adequate or even just. Discuss this point of view.

4. Recount in full the parable of the marriage feast. What warnings would it have for (a) Pharisees; (b) Christians?

5. What is Jesus' teaching on judgment?

17 *The 'Mighty Works' in Matthew and Luke*

We have already seen that the *dunameis* of Jesus recorded in the Gospel of Mark were not 'wonders', forcing men to believe, but 'signs' of the transforming effect of God's compassion and power on the lives of ordinary men and women. The mighty works of the kingdom did not compel belief, but they did force people to think. We have to try to understand what they conveyed to those who saw them, talked about them, and eventually wrote about them.

To Jesus himself they were another way of illustrating the real nature of the kingdom of God. They taught that God's desire for all men and women was physical, mental and spiritual wholeness. By restoring, at considerable risk to himself, a useless hand and paralysed limbs, Jesus showed that healing may depend on another's self-giving service; by healing a leper, he showed that compassion may cleanse another of all that makes him outcast; in opening the eyes of the blind, he demonstrated his power to bring spiritual perception – understanding of the meaning and purpose of life; in helping the woman with the haemorrhage he proved that faith can give new life to the 'dead'.

Jesus' contemporaries summed up all that the mighty works meant to them in the phrase 'the good news'.

In this chapter we shall study the miracles not recorded by Mark.

1. A Miracle Recorded by Both

The centurion's servant (Luke 7.1-10; Matt. 8.5-13)

A centurion was a man of some authority in the army. This one was also well thought of by the Jewish elders because he had built them a synagogue; according to Luke it was they who asked Jesus to heal his slave. (The Palestinian Matthew calls him a servant, not a slave, and omits any mention of Jewish elders being involved with a Gentile army officer; in his account the centurion approached Jesus directly.)

While Jesus was still on his way to the sick man the centurion sent a message that he was not worthy to have the respected healer visit his house, but that he recognized in him an authority which could heal without even seeing or touching the sick person. Faith greater than any Jesus had found among those of his own nation! When the messengers returned to the house they found the slave well.

As with the Syro-Phoenician woman,[1] here too a Gentile's faith is commended – valuable teaching as the church spread out of Palestine and into the wider Graeco-Roman world.

2. A Miracle Recorded only by Matthew

The blind and dumb madman (Matt. 12.22-4; see also 9.32-4)
This healing occasioned the Pharisees' accusation that Jesus healed through the power of Beelzebul the prince of demons.[2] Ordinary people, however, wondered 'Can this be the Son of David?' Had the messiah come at last?

Jesus was unable to use the term messiah of himself because of its political overtones (son of David inevitably suggested a claimant to the throne of Israel and rejection of the Roman Emperor). Instead he ascribed his power to the Spirit of God. John the Baptist had proclaimed that the one he was preparing for would baptize with the Holy Spirit. Now all who had the perception to understand the

---

[1] Chapter 10.2.
[2] The parable of the strong man was Jesus' answer to the accusation: chapter 8.1.

Luke has a healing of a dumb man as the occasion of the Beelzebul controversy (11.14-15). Here we have an example of how an incident could be remembered differently in the various oral traditions. The important thing to those who observed Jesus' mighty works was that God's power was at work; it was relatively unimportant whether the healing that occasioned this understanding was of a multiple sufferer, as in Matthew, or a man who was without the power of speech, as in Luke.

evidence before their own eyes could see the Spirit at work in their midst, and know the power of the presence of God.

3. Miracles Recorded only by Luke

(a) The widow of Nain's son (Luke 7.11-17)

In the healing of Jairus' daughter there had been some doubt as to whether the girl was really dead or, as Jesus himself said, merely sleeping.[3] The widow's son is already on the way to burial. The plight of a childless widow in those days (he was her only son) called out for compassion and practical help.

Jesus spoke to the dead man the same words he had used when he healed the twelve-year-old daughter of Jairus: 'I say to you, arise.' The mourners were filled with awe when the young man sat up and began to speak. Jesus gave him back to his mother. The conviction of those present was that 'a great prophet has arisen among us'. Obviously they were reminded of Elijah's bringing back to life a Gentile widow's son at Zarephath, near Sidon in Phoenicia. Her words to Elijah had been: 'Now I know that you are a man of God, and that the word of the Lord in your mouth is truth.'[4]

To Jairus, ruler of a synagogue and representative of Judaism, Jesus had said, 'Do not fear, only believe.' Do we now see the same concern reaching out to the Gentile world, to give new life and hope there also? Though Nain no longer exists it is thought to have been in Galilee where there was a high percentage of Greeks. A man of God who spoke words of truth would be for them the equivalent of a son of David, the messiah, to Jews.

(b) The crippled woman (Luke 13.10-17)

This healing took place in a synagogue on the sabbath. For eighteen years the woman had been unable to straighten her back. She did not approach Jesus herself, nor did anyone speak on her behalf as in the healings of Jairus' daughter, the Syro-Phoenician woman's daughter, the paralysed man, the epileptic boy, and the centurion's

---

[3] Chapter 9.4.
[4] 1 Kings 17.8-24. There is a similar story of Elisha and the Shunammite's son in 2 Kings 4.8-37. What we call 'the kiss of life' seems to have revived both boys. If this is so, those resuscitations are quite different from what Jesus did with the young man at Nain.

servant; when he saw her he had been filled with compassion. Jesus knew that the synagogue ruler would not hesitate to untie his animals and give them water on the sabbath; why then did he hypocritically deny healing on the sabbath to a fellow human being? On another occasion he said that as the sabbath had been given for man's benefit it was right to do good on it.[5]

(c) The man with dropsy (Luke 14.1-6)

Dropsy is a painful and incapacitating condition in which fluid collects in the body, particularly the feet and legs, because of the weakness of the heart's pumping action.

This is another sabbath healing. It took place not in a synagogue but in the house of a synagogue ruler who belonged to the Pharisee sect, whose extreme, legalistic interpretation of the sabbath forbade medical care except when life was in danger. Jesus healed the man, and then reminded his silent critics with some sharpness that they would act quickly enough to save an animal of their own that happened to fall into a well on the sabbath. Oxen and asses were valuable possessions; was it financial self-interest that motivated them?

(d) The ten lepers (Luke 17.11-19)

Jesus was passing between Samaria and Galilee on the way to Jerusalem when ten lepers asked for help. Priests had to certify that a one-time leper was quite cured before he could return to his village and the society of healthy people. When they saw that they had been cured only one, a Samaritan, ran back to give thanks. Jesus assured him that his faith had made him well, just as he had the woman with the haemorrhage and Bartimaeus.[6]

Like the other healings of non-Jews: the centurion's servant, the Syro-Phoenician woman's daughter and, probably, the Gerasene demoniac, the deaf and dumb man of the Decapolis, and the son of the widow of Nain, this evidence of the Lord's love and concern going out to men of all races indiscriminately was proof that Jesus was not merely messiah of the Jews but saviour of the world.

[5] Mark 2.27; 3.4.
[6] Faith had also been a factor in the healing of the paralysed man, the centurion's servant, the Syro-Phoenician woman's daughter, and the epileptic boy though, in those cases, it was the faith of those who had brought the sick person's need before the Lord.

Jesus drew attention to the fact that of the ten it was the 'foreigner' alone who had returned to praise God for his healing. The Pharisees and others who were self-righteous about the superiority of their worship and devotion should not despise the faith of Samaritans, but rather learn from the immediate response of this man.

REVISION QUESTIONS

1. Describe one healing when Jesus was asked by another to heal the sufferer, and one in which he healed without being asked.

2. Which healings of all those you have studied mention faith as a factor in the healing? What role do you think faith might play in healing?

3. Describe briefly the healings of non-Jews. Why would the evangelists be particularly interested in these?

4. Tell either the story of the healing of the centurion's servant (slave) or the raising of the widow's son.

5. Which healings gave rise to criticism that Jesus broke the sabbath? How did he answer the criticism? (To make sure that you are familiar with all Jesus' healings, revise chapters 6.2; 9.2,3,4; 10.2,3; 11.1,4,6.

18 *The Sermon on the Mount: Guidance in Decision-Making*

Matt. 5-7

As we saw in chapter 2, Jesus' teaching was preserved for many years in the minds and hearts of those who had heard him speak and had seen how he lived. It was the needs of the growing Christian community which led in time to the writing down of these memories and ultimately to their incorporation in the gospels. A generation or two elapsed between gospel and the gospels. By the time the gospels were actually written the circumstances surrounding any one saying of Jesus had long been forgotten: it was *what* the master had said that was important, not where, when or to whom. The evangelists had to use as they thought best the often quite short paragraphs of Jesus' teaching that had come down to them, and they arranged them in the way that would best bring out for their readers the essential meaning of the gospel.

When Matthew came to write his gospel he wanted to incorporate those sayings which were a guide in the decision-making of everyday life. Since those for whom he was writing had hitherto found such guidance in the law given by Moses at Mount Sinai, Matthew arranged Jesus' teaching in a way that would suggest that it fulfilled and reinterpreted the Mosaic law.

This 'sermon on the mount', as it is called, seems to be one long instruction by Jesus to his disciples and the crowds gathered on a mountain-side, but it is Matthew's own arrangement of what Jesus had taught on many different occasions to the men and women he met as he travelled around Palestine in the first century AD. Their environment was vastly different from ours; their moral code, their customs, their problems are largely foreign to us. Yet Jesus' knowledge of human nature has meant that much of what he said then is still relevant today.

The sermon on the mount is not a set of rules or a code of behaviour, but a 'design for living' which offers guidance on how to live a fulfilling and satisfying life.

Luke has some of this teaching in a shorter 'sermon on the plain' (6.20-49), and other sayings found in the sermon on the mount appear here and there throughout the Gospel arranged according to Luke's plan.

Matthew's 'design for living' in chapters 5-7 begins with eight statements on the characteristics which make for real and lasting happiness, the happiness of the kingdom of heaven. Then comes a reinterpretation of two of the ten commandments and three other ancient Israelite laws to illustrate the importance of motive in human behaviour. Next is advice on building an honest relationship with God. The fourth section concerns responsibility towards oneself and others. Finally, the teaching of the sermon on the mount is summed up as 'the way that leads to life'.

1. The Beatitudes

Matt. 5.1-16; Luke 6.20-26

The beatitudes are so called because each begins in the Latin translation with *beata*, blessed, or happy. The poetic parallelism is even more marked in the original Aramaic, and would ensure their being easily remembered by those who heard them from Jesus' lips.

Luke has four 'beatitudes' and four 'woes' which put in a negative way what the beatitudes express positively.

Because some of the words now mean something quite different to us (for example, 'meek', 'poor in spirit'), the following notes are intended as a guide to the original meaning.

Jesus said that happiness comes to those:

(i) who are neither self-important nor over-bearing towards others ('poor in spirit');

(ii) who grieve over the sin and suffering of others ('who mourn');

(iii) who are God-controlled rather than self-seeking: they seem 'meek' because they are not grabbing aggressively for themselves, but they are in fact the strong who will 'inherit the earth';

(iv) who hunger and thirst for a world in which love and justice ('righteousness') prevail in society and between individuals (hunger and thirst are probably the strongest motivation a human being can have to make him act);

(v) who are merciful: generous to others' weaknesses, and forgiving;

(vi) who are straightforward and singleminded ('pure in heart');

(vii) who are reconcilers: helping both parties in a dispute to understand each other, and working to mend broken relationships whether personal or social, racial or religious or national;

(viii) who are persecuted (or slandered or ridiculed) for Christ's sake yet continue to live by their beliefs.

The beatitudes set a tremendous ideal, an ideal which some have said is unattainable. That may be, but there is a deep need in human beings for a worthwhile goal to strive towards. The goal may be climbing Mount Everest or finding a cure for cancer or solving the world problem of poverty or merely living up to the best that is in us. Jesus said that people who try to live by such ideals are 'the salt of the earth' and 'the light of the world' because they preserve and make known in it a quality of life which is the real glory of creation.

2. Reinterpretation of the Law – Intention and Motive
Matt. 5.17-48; Luke 6.27-36

St Paul called the law of Moses a teacher preparing the world for the coming of Christ; once he had come its work was done.[1] Matthew wanted to assure his Palestinian Jewish friends that Jesus was not a destroyer of the law as the Pharisees and scribes had feared; rather had he brought out its true meaning and purpose. This purpose had still to be accomplished, but it could not be achieved by the Pharisees' legalistic observance. It was not that Jesus set a lower standard; in fact he told his followers that 'unless your righteousness exceeds that of the scribes and Pharisees, you will never enter the kingdom of heaven'.

The following examples of his reinterpretation of the old show

[1] Galatians 3.24. The word Paul used is that from which our word *pedagogue* (schoolmaster) comes. In the RSV it has been translated by the word 'guardian'.

just how much more demanding was his new teaching.

(a) Killing and anger (Matt. 5.21-6)

The sixth commandment said 'you shall not kill'. Jesus said that anger was like murder if allowed to rankle and destroy relationships. Reconciliation, making up a quarrel, must come even before 'offering your gift at the altar' in worship.

(b) Adultery and lust (Matt. 5.27-32; Luke 16.18)

The seventh commandment laid down that 'you shall not commit adultery'. Jesus held that lust could be as destructive as adultery, and that divorcing one's marriage partner may force him or her into adultery.

Sexual relationships seem private, but in fact they are never private because they always affect others. Each person has a responsibility to face honestly the full consequences of sexual behaviour, including adultery, lust and divorce.

Mark and Luke omit the words 'except for unchastity', making the warning against divorce more absolute. There may be some marriages which have so completely broken down that there is no alternative to divorce; but this does not cancel what Jesus was setting before his disciples: a respect for the other person as being as valuable and as vulnerable as we ourselves are and a responsibility for his or her welfare.[2]

(c) Oaths and truthfulness (Matt. 5.33-7)

The law condemned the making of an oath when the swearer intended to tell a lie. Jesus said that if the simple truth were always told, all oaths would become unnecessary.

(d) Retaliation and non-resistance (Matt. 5.38-42; Luke 6.29-30)

Moses had limited retribution to an 'eye for eye, tooth for tooth',[3] and this was a humane advance on the earlier unrestricted blood-feuds in retaliation for even unintentional injuries. Jesus' teaching forbade all revenge.

'Turn the other cheek' sounds like foolishness but it is in fact the

---

[2] There is further teaching on divorce in Matt. 19.1-12; see also chapter 11.5(v).

[3] As for example in Lev. 24.20.

only way to prevent violence escalating. Ghandi and Martin Luther King have proved this in modern times.

The men of the kingdom were to be generous of their possessions, their time, and their money.

(e) Hatred and love (Matt. 5.43-8; Luke 6.27-8,32-6)

The old covenant obliged members of Israel to love their neighbours and it meant by this only fellow-Israelites, men of the same race and religion and country. Jesus' followers were to love even their enemies and persecutors. He had had plenty of both so he knew what he was asking. His reason was that we are all children of a loving Father and should be as generous in forgiving, loving, and in serving others as God is, thus co-operating with him in making the world a place in which all men, women and children can find the health and wholeness necessary to fulfil the potential of their human nature.

The Greek word translated 'perfect' means 'fulfilling an end'. To live lovingly is to fulfil the purpose of creation.

3. Relationship with God
Matt. 6.1-21

If relationship with God is to be a living influence, it must be without pretence. Once again the importance of motive and intention is stressed.

(a) Almsgiving (Matt. 6.1-4)

Good deeds are a kind of prayer when the motive is to help those in need, not to impress.

(b) Prayer (Matt. 6.5-8)

Empty gestures and words are not prayer. Prayer is communion with God, whether it is expressed by means of words or in the silent adoration of the heart.

(c) Pattern for Christian prayer (Matt. 6.9-15; Luke 11.2-4)

Jesus gave his disciples a model for their own prayer:
  (i) God is to be held in reverence.

(ii) The coming of the kingdom is to be prayed for.

(iii) What is prayed for must also be worked for: 'thy will be done' in me, through me, by me.

(iv) Forgiveness must be given and received for all that has gone wrong in our lives so that a new start becomes possible.

(v) Strength in temptation and protection from evil are to be prayed for.

For thine is the kingdom, the power, and the glory: for ever and ever is not found in the earliest manuscripts of the New Testament. These words are called 'the doxology' because they give glory (*doxa* in Greek) to God. They were added to the Lord's Prayer when it began to be used in public worship.

(d) Fasting (Matt. 6.16-18)

The Pharisees fasted twice a week, on Mondays and Thursdays, and put ashes on their heads and looked gloomy so that all would know they were fasting and be impressed by their piety. Jesus said that fasting, like almsgiving and prayer, was an offering of worship only when it was sincerely done with that intention.

The word 'hypocrite' comes from the Greek word for the mask which actors donned to indicate the part they were playing on the stage. We should not act a part towards God.

(e) True treasure (Matt. 6.19-21; Luke 12.33-4)

Although everything in God's creation is good in itself, we can become slaves of our possessions. Rather should we seek to build up true and lasting values within ourselves.

4. Responsibility towards Oneself and Others
Matt. 6.22—7.12

Throughout our lives we have to make choices between two or more courses of action, and between the many different attitudes we might adopt in any particular situation. If the principles on which our attitudes and decisions are based are informed by the light of the gospel, then our lives will be full of light. If, however, our 'inner light' is darkness, our lives as a whole will be filled with darkness. It is impossible to follow opposite and contradictory ways of living: 'You cannot serve God and mammon.'

(a) Anxiety (Matt. 6.25-34; Luke 12.22-32)

The fact that choices have to be made, and that the choices each individual makes affect, to some extent, other human beings, gives rise to anxiety. Jesus said that there is no need for anxiety because God can be trusted to bring good out of any situation. He was not referring to sensible planning and foresight, but to the kind of anxiety which paralyses effort and robs of all sense of security. Such anxiety is really lack of trust. He is saying that if God is sought first, all else falls into place.

(b) Judging (Matt. 7.1-5; Luke 6.37-8,41-2)

There is a temptation to judge or criticize those whose choices in life are different from one's own. Jesus said that no one is in a position to judge another since it is impossible to know fully intention and motive behind behaviour, nor to understand the temptations that another has to fight. Sometimes the faults of others are in reality our own blindness: the faults we think we see do not exist in reality, they are the 'log' that is in our own eye. Often those who criticize others remain blind to much greater faults in themselves. The use of the words 'log' and 'speck' suggest that Jesus may have first given this teaching to timber-cutters or carpenters.

'The measure you give will be the measure you get' is similar teaching to that of the parable of the unmerciful servant on forgiveness, and of the parable of the sheep and goats on mercy. Those who are merciful and forgiving, will themselves receive mercy and forgiveness.

(c) Pearls before swine (Matt. 7.6)

It is difficult to understand what place this saying might have had in Jesus' teaching.

It may have seemed like a warning against betraying Christianity to pagans in times of persecution, and have been included by Matthew for this reason. It may also be a warning against unwise and premature evangelism: do not force your beliefs on others before they are able to understand their value.

(d) Ask ... seek ... knock (Matt. 7.7-11; Luke 11.9-13)

Ask ... Seek ... Knock. God desires to give 'good things'. Prayer is answered – though perhaps not as we wanted; God gives only that which is for our *real* good.

(e) The golden rule (Matt. 7.12; Luke 6.31)

A disciple's obligation towards others is summed up by 'whatever you wish that men would do to you, do so to them.' This had been the teaching of the law and the prophets of Hebrew religion, and it was another way of expressing the new law of love of the new Israel: 'You shall love your neighbour *as yourself.*' Not only should disciples treat others lovingly but they should have a proper respect and love for themselves.

5. *The Way into Life*
Matt. 7.13-29

(a) The narrow gate (Matt. 7.13-14; Luke 13.23-4)

This saying recalls the discipleship-teaching of the journey to Jerusalem: the necessity for accepting and facing life's difficulties, for being willing to lose one's self-centred life, for some discipline and self-denial so that one's character and personality is not maimed by over-indulgence of some one instinct or desire.

Facing difficult choices rather than evading them is the hard way – but it is the way that leads to fulness of life.

(b) The good tree that bears good fruit (Matt. 7.15-20; Luke 6.43-5)

Just as the quality of the fruit is an indication of the value of the tree from which it comes, so also a man's actions and attitudes reveal the person behind them.

'False prophets' is an expression used by the church in Matthew's own day of those teachers whose words or behaviour were destroying the gospel of love and wholeness. Matthew probably had some of these in mind as he thought about Jesus' saying: since their 'fruit' was evil so must they be also. Jesus' words thus became a warning to the young church: 'Beware of false prophets ...'

(c) The will of the Father (Matt. 7.21-3; Luke 8.21; 11.28)

It is not words, claims to be religious or to do good works, which will gain the kingdom, but only doing the will of God.

(d) Parable of the two houses (Matt. 7.24-7; Luke 6.47-9)

The sermon ends with a warning to those who take pleasure in listening to the gospel, but do not let it influence or change their lives. It is only by *doing*, by putting into practice the word of God as revealed in the life of Jesus, that their foundations will be dug deep enough to withstand the storms and doubts which must inevitably come. Those who merely hear the gospel and do nothing about it will find their faith as frail as a house built on sand: when the gales blow and the floods rise (when troubles and temptations come) it will fail them.

There is another saying in Luke which stresses the importance of acting out in one's daily life what one professes to believe: 'No one who puts his hand to the plough and looks back is fit for the kingdom of God' (Luke 9.57-62).

(e) The authority for this teaching (Matt. 7.28-9)

Many different individuals and groups had been struck with the authority with which Jesus spoke. It was a personal authority: it did not depend on man-made laws. Matthew believed that anyone could test out this authority for himself. He believed that by living as Jesus did and taught, any human being would find himself growing in wholeness and fulness of life. That is, Jesus' teaching was self-authenticating: it proved itself – this is the real measure of his authority for asking others to follow him, and for all that he said and did.

REVISION QUESTIONS

1. It has been said that the value of Jesus Christ's teaching is that he lived it out in his own life. What is there in his life to illustrate his teaching on forgiveness of enemies and mercy in judging others?

2. What did he teach about the importance of motive or in-

tention in human behaviour? What do you think was his own motive and intention for living as he did?

3. Briefly state the eight beatitudes. What value have they for life today? Illustrate your answer by reference to real-life situations.

4. What did Jesus teach about relationships with others? (Use any parable or saying.)

19   *Prayer and Forgiveness*

1. Prayer

How are we to account for the power which so many different groups of people – Jew and Gentile, childless widow and Roman centurion, demoniac and lawyer – acknowledged in the one they came to call the Christ? 'Holy one of God', 'Son of the Most High God', 'a man of authority', 'messiah', 'a great prophet', 'Son of God', are attempts to express their conviction that he had something which other men had not.[1] How are we to account for this 'extra something'? The voice from heaven had called him 'my beloved Son with whom I am well pleased', and told the three apostles to 'listen to him'.[2] How was it that he was able to speak 'the word of the Lord'?

The synoptic gospels reveal Jesus as a man of prayer. The intimacy of his prayer-relationship with God is obvious from his use of the Aramaic *Abba*, father, as his name for God. His conviction of the rightness of his mission to the world is rooted in the unbroken sense of communion – union-with-God (Matt. 11.27; Luke 10.22).

Luke in particular portrays Jesus at prayer in all the crucial moments of his life: at his baptism; when reports of his healings first began to attract people in large numbers; before choosing the twelve; before asking the question at Caesarea Philippi which would tell him if the time had come to prepare the disciples for his death; when Peter, James and John had the vision of his transfigured glory; in the garden of Gethsemane as he waited to be arrested; on the cross.[3]

[1] Mark 1.24; 5.7; Matt. 8.5f.; Mark 8.29; Luke 7.16; Mark 15.39.
[2] Mark 1.11 and 9.7.
[3] Luke 3.21; 5.15-16; 6.12; 9.18-22; 9.29; 22.41f; 23.46.

He prayed for others; because he was aware of both Peter's weakness and potential strength, he prayed that Peter's faith would not fail in temptation and that he would ultimately become a strength to others.[4] He told the disciples to pray for themselves that they might not be overcome by temptation.[5] 'Watch and pray' was his general advice.[6]

Luke saw in Jesus' life of prayer the continuing source of his power to reveal God to men, and to bring about the reign – the *basileia* (kingdom) – of God on earth.

Luke was not the first to sense that the secret of Jesus' authority lay in his closeness to God through prayer. The disciples had asked him to teach them to pray (Luke 11.1). In this chapter we shall consider Jesus' teaching on prayer, for he did expect men to pray and he set before them as their model his own Father-Son relationship with God (Luke 11.2). We shall see that as well as this pattern-prayer he used parables and his own example to encourage them to persevere. Since he spoke of forgiveness as a pre-requisite for prayer (both one's own forgiveness by God and one's forgiving others), we shall include his three parables of forgiveness and the stories of the sinful woman and Zacchaeus which demonstrate its effect in a human life.

(a) The Lord's prayer (Luke 11.2-4; Matt. 6.9-13)

In the synoptic gospels we have two versions of what Christians call 'the Lord's Prayer'. Matthew's version is the most familiar one. It expands the basic guidelines of Luke's shorter outline or pattern for all Christian prayer. Probably Jesus was asked by different people on many occasions for help in their striving to live close to God and his replies on at least two such occasions have come down to us.[7]

When we analyse the Lord's Prayer we see that it speaks of one's attitude to God, responsibility for praying that his kingdom will come, concern for the material needs of the world, the necessity for forgiveness, and for help in temptations.

(i) Jesus took it for granted that men would want to pray: that

[4] Luke 22.32.
[5] Luke 22.40.
[6] Luke 21.36.
[7] Matthew's version is treated briefly in chapter 18.3(c).

is, live in relationship with God. He taught that the remote Creator-God, whom men up till then had feared more than loved, was close to each of his children and cared about their welfare. Although involved in the world, he was still the transcendent God worthy of adoration and worship and this must be the first element in Christian prayer. 'Name' means the character and being of God – God as he really is in himself.

(ii) We should pray for his reign in the hearts of all mankind. Jesus believed that only when God's kingdom had fully come would there be justice and mercy and brotherhood in society, and consequently the possibility of wholeness and holiness and health for individuals.

(iii) By praying for 'our' daily bread we acknowledge our solidarity with all other human beings and pledge ourselves to work to make this prayer come true for the starving. The world's resources could supply the basic needs of all if justly shared.

(iv) Elsewhere are Jesus' words: 'Forgive, so that your Father may forgive you' (Mark 11.25); and his warning that a man should be reconciled with his 'brother' before coming to God in worship (Matt. 5.23-6). There is a universal human need for forgiveness because sin and guilt erect barriers of fear and hatred between man and man, and man and God. Unless there is forgiveness for others in our hearts, we are unable to receive the forgiveness we ourselves need. Hardness of heart is damaging to ourselves, as well as to those we refuse to forgive.

(v) Temptation is inevitable throughout life, and facing it brings growth in maturity. But sometimes temptations can be too strong to cope with alone; Jesus recommended prayer that we should not be overcome by temptation.

(b) Parable of the friend at midnight (Luke 11.5-13)

This parable and the saying that follows it teach two points about prayer: God is ready to answer, and we should be persistent prayers. God is contrasted with the reluctant friend who nevertheless responded to persistent knocking: 'How much more will the heavenly Father give the Holy Spirit to those who ask him.' The poetical form of vv.9-10 would make this teaching easily remembered.

The Holy Spirit came to Jesus at his baptism, and was with him as he agonized over the way he was to fulfil his vocation of sonship. and as he began his teaching in Galilee. It was the presence of the Holy Spirit that enabled him to heal.[8] He was the one who would 'baptize' others with the Holy Spirit.[9] By asking for the Holy Spirit (Matthew has 'good things') we shall have all that is needed: the Spirit brings both God's presence, and the power to act in the best possible way in each situation.

Similar teaching on the readiness of God to answer prayer, and the power of the faith that lies behind the desire to pray, is found in Mark 11.22-4: 'Have faith in God ... whatever you ask in prayer, believe that you receive it, and you will.' A saying recorded by Matthew is that faith moves mountains (Matt. 17.20). The apostles once asked Jesus to 'Increase our faith!' and his reply showed that he believed faith opened to us enormous resources of power (Luke 17.5-6).

(c) Parable of the unjust judge (Luke 18.1-8)

God is again contrasted with the figure in the parable. The teaching is that we should trust God and 'pray and not lose heart'. The 'reluctant friend' and 'unjust judge' startle us into thinking about the subject of prayer.[10] If God knows our needs before we pray we ask, why pray?[11]

Prayer is not magic; it does not change God's mind or talk him into doing something that he would not otherwise have done. But it does change the one who prays. To pray is to offer oneself as a channel through which God's love and power may become effective in the world around. Prayer builds up a relationship with God in which human nature may be transformed into the quality seen in Jesus Christ.

(d) The lesson of the epileptic boy (Mark 9.14-29; Matt. 17.14-21; Luke 9.37-43)

The relevance of this incident to the subject of prayer is made clear in the last verse in Matthew and Mark's account.

[8] Luke 3.22; 4.1; 4.14-15; Matt. 12.28.
[9] Luke 3.16.
[10] The reason why Jesus used parables is discussed in chapter 8, p. 45.
[11] Matt. 6.8; Luke 12.22-32.

(e) Jesus' prayer at Gethsemane (Mark 14.32-42; Matt. 26.36-46; Luke 22.39-46)

Jesus' prayer at Gethsemane was both a request to God to save him from suffering and an expression of his willingness to be used in whatever way was necessary to help others: '... yet not what I will, but what thou wilt.' This heartfelt prayer was repeated over and over until he had found courage, peace of mind, and strength to face whatever the future held.

The incident of the epileptic boy taught that the power to help others would come through prayer. Now we see that strength to cope with one's own situation may also come through prayer. (Although the parable of the Pharisee and the publican has been included in the following section on forgiveness, it does in fact teach the need for reality in prayer: that a man must face himself honestly and admit his need for repentance.)

2. Forgiveness

(a) Parable of the Pharisee and publican (Luke 18.9-14)

The different approach to God of these two men shows that facing the truth about oneself (humility) and wanting to change what is wrong in one's life (repentance) are both necessary before one can receive forgiveness.

Because the publican (from *publicanus*, latin for tax collector) saw his need for help, he could be forgiven and enabled to make a new start. Because the Pharisee would not see himself as he really was, and was too proud to admit any need for change, he was unable to receive forgiveness.

(b) Parable of the unmerciful servant (Matt. 18.21-35)

Since God's forgiveness is unlimited, so must ours be of our fellow-men, and sincere from the heart.

Ten thousand talents is such an enormous sum (something like £5,000,000) that the official was probably a provincial governor responsible for the revenues of a province. Although he asked for time to pay, it would have been quite impossible for him to save up such a sum. A hundred denarii, on the other hand, was a comparatively small sum, and could have been easily repaid in time.

(c) Parable of the two sons (Matt. 21.28-32)

The teaching of this parable is that it is repentance that counts. Because the first son was humble enough to think it possible that he might be in the wrong and honest enough to let others know he had changed his mind, he could, like the tax collector and the prodigal son, be forgiven. The second son was like the Pharisee in that he thought he could do no wrong.

Jesus told this parable against the chief priests and elders of the temple who would not admit that they had been wrong to use the temple as a market (Matt. 21.12-13,23,31). He said that harlots and tax collectors who repented when a better way of life was put before them would go into the kingdom before the outwardly respectable and religious people who were, in reality, full of pride and pretence. Real sinners had listened to John the Baptist; those who thought themselves 'righteous' had not.

(d) The sinful woman (Luke 7.36-50)

Words are not always necessary to show our desire for repentance and forgiveness. Jesus' host had omitted all the customary courtesies which he should have shown to a guest. He had not provided water to bathe the hot and dusty feet of the traveller, nor oil to counteract the drying effects of the sun. The loving attention of the 'woman of the city' (the phrase suggests a prostitute) in making up for the Pharisee's rudeness was her way of showing that she wanted to abandon her past life; her faith in Jesus' willingness to accept her despite her sinful past is what saved her. He said that one who loves much can be forgiven much.

(e) Zacchaeus (Luke 19.1-10)

The woman had demonstrated her repentance and then received forgiveness. Zacchaeus repented as a result of the friendship offered him by Jesus (see v.10).

Like Levi, Zacchaeus was a social outcast because of his occupation; as a *chief* tax collector, he would have been even more despised. He had probably become a rich man by extorting a little extra 'tax' for his own pocket. Perhaps Jesus' gesture of acceptance was the first ever shown him.

Unless a man lives as he speaks, his words will carry no conviction. What is of particular value about the teaching of Jesus Christ is that it was seen in practice in his life. Men knew that it worked. When he asked his disciples to preach repentance and forgiveness of sins,[12] they did so because they had seen the effect such teaching had had in the lives of men and women like Zacchaeus and the woman in the Pharisee's house. When he said that their forgiveness of others should be unlimited,[13] they accepted it as their own ideal to strive after because they had once seen a paralysed man walk when the burden of guilt was lifted from him. When Jesus expected those who followed him to pray, they did so because they knew that his own prayer-relationship with God was the vital force in his life. They were willing to listen, believing that the words he spoke were truth, because Jesus the Christ lived as he prayed – in the Father's presence.

REVISION QUESTIONS

1. What do the synoptic gospels reveal of Jesus' own practice of prayer and worship?

2. What did Jesus teach on the subject of prayer? Illustrate your answer with references to the parables and the sermon on the mount.

3. Why is forgiveness important? Relate one parable which is concerned with men's forgiveness of each other, and an incident in which Jesus forgave a sinner.

4. What is the connection between repentance and forgiveness? What parables and incidents from the ministry of Jesus demonstrate this connection?

[12] Luke 24.27.
[13] Matt. 18.21-2; Luke 17.3-4.

20 *The Birth Narratives*

Matt. 1–2; Luke 1–2

1. *Why End at the Beginning?*

By studying Jesus' life and teaching before Matthew and Luke's birth narratives we are putting ourselves in the same situation as the first Christians. They became interested in Jesus' origins only because they had already found significance in his life and death. The good news came first and interest in biographical details much later when people began to wonder why it was that his life was different from other men's. Because his followers had experienced the presence of the risen Lord and knew that his Spirit was in their midst,[1] they began to ask if there was anything in his early life which might explain his power to give new life to others.

This pattern is reflected in the gospels. The earliest, Mark, begins with the adult man entering upon his life's work. The dramatic note of Matthew 3.1 could be the beginning of an earlier draft of the Gospel of Matthew, and Luke 3.1 suggests the opening sentence of a Greek work with its precise dating of the events about to be narrated. There is reason to think that both originally began at the same point as Mark, and that the chapters on Jesus' birth were added subsequently as if offering an explanation of his life: he was overshadowed by the Holy Spirit from the moment of his conception.

This is an important point. If the wonders associated with the birth had been widely known,[2] expectation of further wonders

---

[1] Luke 24.49; Acts 2; 3.6,16.
[2] The earliest New Testament writings, Paul's letters, do not mention Jesus' birth, and neither does the Gospel according to John.

might have coloured the record of his adult ministry. Since men knew his mighty works, and the greatest of them, the resurrection, first and only later learnt about his birth, there is no reason to think that the gospel record is biased.

2. The Nature and Aim of the Birth Stories

The imagery and symbolism of Matthew 1-2 and Luke 1-2 is strange to us. These chapters are trying to express what cannot be easily conveyed in ordinary language: the belief that the power of God was uniquely present in the life of Christ. Our concern is with the reality behind the symbolism, just as it is when we use mathematical formulae and written music. The sharps and flats and lines and notes of a music score are meaningless apart from the musical pitches they notate. Similarly, when we read of the overshadowing of the Holy Spirit and of angel messengers and of wise men led by a star we must allow this symbolic language to convey its truth in its own way. It is not the language of our everyday experience or of logical argument, and it is not meant to be analysed as they must be. It is trying to express what is beyond sensory experience and thought.

Nevertheless, the logical language of the gospels and the poetry of the birth stories are conveying the same truth in their so different ways. The Christian gospel is that God has made himself known through Jesus Christ. This is expressed in the language of the creeds: '... I believe in one Lord Jesus Christ ... incarnate by the Holy Ghost of the Virgin Mary ...' Christian belief in the incarnation (literally, 'taking flesh') is that Jesus the son of Mary is the incarnate Son of God.

3. Luke's Account: Preparation
Luke 1

(a) Purpose (Luke 1.1-4)

Where did Luke get his information about Jesus' birth and boyhood? Why did he write about it? He claimed in his introductory verses that the source of his information was '... those who from the beginning were eyewitnesses and ministers of the word', and that his intention was '... to write an orderly account ... that you may know the truth concerning the things of which you have been informed'. That is, Luke claims to have firsthand information, and he intends to make the truth known.

Although Luke's own background is that of a non-Jew living in a Greek cultural environment, he portrays accurately Palestinian Jewish religious and family customs. His information must have come to him from someone who lived in the same sort of villages as Bethlehem or Nazareth. Tradition says it came from Mary herself or from someone close to her in whom she had confided.

But Luke's style of writing in these first two chapters is very different from his writing up of the eyewitness material in the rest of his gospel. The birth stories are in the language not of history but of poetry and worship. The kind of truth Luke wanted to convey by means of his birth narrative was religious truth: that the events of the Christian gospel can be understood only when they are seen as the activity of God.

(b) The promise of John's birth (Luke 1.5-25)

The name John means 'God is gracious'. Gabriel, the name the angel introduced himself by, means 'man of God'. A Nazarite was one dedicated to God's service at birth.

At that time God was held in such awe that it was thought impossible that he would approach a human being directly: he used messengers, *angelos* in Greek. We no longer expect him to speak through angels; our experience is that we somehow come to know what he wants us to do with our lives through our own thinking and reflecting on the events of everyday life and the words of other human beings which have the power to illuminate life's meaning and purpose for us.

Elizabeth and Zechariah were both descended from the ancient priestly family of Aaron, and were representative of the best in Hebrew religion. When their son grew to manhood he was hailed as a prophet in the tradition of the great Elijah. John is the culmination of the religion of the old covenant between God and the chosen people; his life's work was to be the preparation of his people for the *new* covenant: 'Repent, for the kingdom of God is at hand ...'

(c) Annunciation to Mary (Luke 1.26-38)

Jesus is a form of the Hebrew name Joshua which means 'God is salvation' or 'God will save'. Betrothal was a formal contract which custom dictated should last a year. In those days and in that culture men believed that God was involved in every conception of a new human life; Luke and Matthew both say that Jesus was conceived by the *direct* intervention of God, i.e. without the agency of a human father. This belief is known as 'the virgin birth', but it would be more accurately described as a virginal conception. Although Joseph is referred to as Jesus' father (Luke 2.23; 4.22), the birth narratives also say that Mary was a virgin at the time of his conception (see the words in brackets in Luke 3.23; Matt. 1.25; and Mary's words to Gabriel, Luke 1.34).

There have always been Christians who have found it difficult to believe that Jesus was not conceived in the normal way, and of course there is no reason why the incarnation should be dependent on a virginal conception. The religious truth which the stories of the annunciation and virgin birth convey is that when human beings respond to God's presence (his over-shadowing of their human nature), a new quality of human living becomes a possibility. This is the importance of the virgin birth.

The majority of Christians have, however, believed that Jesus' conception was supernatural, that he had no human father. It is necessary to be clear about the distinction between the virgin birth and the incarnation. The former refers to the *manner* of Jesus' conception, the latter to the fundamental Christian belief that God has revealed himself in Jesus Christ.

(d) Mary's visit to Elizabeth (Luke 1.39-56)

In reporting Elizabeth's own words of greeting, Luke conveys poetically the attitude of the adult John to Jesus, and of Christians to his mother, rather than the response of a baby in the womb. The adult John recognized Jesus as the Lord, and Christians respected Mary as his mother.

Mary's reply to Elizabeth is in the form of a Jewish psalm, and has some similarities with Hannah's song in I Samuel 2.1-10:

known as *Magnificat* from the first word of the Latin translation, it became part of Christian worship in the early days of the church. It may have been a Jewish hymn of thanksgiving for God's saving acts throughout Israel's history which Mary used to express her own gratitude to God, or which Luke has adopted to demonstrate the Christian belief that the birth of Mary's child was the greatest of God's saving acts.

We do not know whether Mary's return home after her three month's visit was just before or just after John's birth.

(e) The birth of John the Baptist (Luke 1.57-80)

It is Jewish custom to circumcise and name a boy on the eighth day after birth. When Elizabeth gave the baby's name her neighbours and relations were surprised because it was not a family name. Zechariah had been dumb ever since he had doubted the truth of his spiritual experience in the temple (Luke 1.8-22); now, with his acceptance of the name then given him for his son, he was able to speak again. The events surrounding John's birth caused a stir throughout the hill country of Judea and people wondered what John would be when he grew up since it seemed that God's hand was on him in a special way. Apparently he lived in the wilderness before he began his call to repentance and preparation for the coming of the Lord; perhaps his parents, already advanced in years when he was born, had died and left him alone in the world, or else he chose such solitude the better to think out his vocation.

Zechariah's thanksgiving for all that had happened, just as the angel had foretold, is also expressed in the form of a psalm which became part of Christian worship. Known as *Benedictus*, it recalls God's promises through the centuries, and the response of his people in a service of love, holiness and righteousness without fear.

4. Luke's Account: Expectation Fulfilled

Luke 2

(a) The birth of Jesus (Luke 2.1-20)

The first Roman Emperor had introduced the census as a means of recording the resources of the Roman Empire. Joseph had to go to his tribal city, Bethlehem (he was a distant descendant of King

David), and although they were not yet married Mary went with him because it was nearly time for her confinement. The town was so crowded that they could get no accommodation in the inn and the baby's first cradle had to be an animal's food-trough.

The expressions 'Saviour' and 'Christ the Lord' are from the church's worship in Luke's day. The angel's song conveys the awe with which he and others thought of the incarnation, of God's intimate relationship with human existence through Christ. As we have already noted, it is virtually impossible to write of a past event without one's present understanding of it determining the language one uses.

(b) Circumcision (Luke 2.21)

The name Jesus, God saves, expresses exactly what Christ's disciples knew to be true from their own experience. They had seen him in his earthly life healing men and women from all that maimed their lives. They had found a new wholeness through their relationship with the master and with one another in the fellowship which had gathered around him. They had come, through him, to a healing and re-creating relationship with God. That Jesus Christ was indeed 'Saviour' was the conviction of the first Christians. The name 'Jesus' expressed the reality which they had experienced in their own lives.

(c) Presentation in the temple (Luke 2.22-40)

The Jewish law prescribed the offering of a first-born son to God. This 'presentation' was connected with the custom of 'purification' when a woman gave thanks for the safe delivery of her child and herself from the dangers (in those days) of childbirth. Since Jerusalem was but six miles from Bethlehem, Mary and Joseph were able to go to the temple for these ceremonies. He who was to be recognized later as the 'fulfilment of the law and the prophets' did, as a child, fulfil the requirements of the law.

Simeon's song of thanksgiving is known as Nunc Dimittis, and reflects the belief that Gentiles, too, will find the light of God's revelation through the Christ. However, Simeon knew that salvation would not come without suffering: there is always human opposition to God's purposes; and he spoke of the agony Mary would undergo.

Simeon and Anna, an old woman whom Luke describes as a prophetess, represent the men and women of Israel who had looked for God's redemption of Jerusalem. Perhaps Luke has mentioned them because they are evidence that some at least within Judaism recognized Jesus as the fulfilment of prophecy and priesthood as well as of the ancient law.

Joseph and Mary returned to their own village of Nazareth in Galilee and there Jesus grew up, strong and wise, to learn Joseph's trade of carpenter.

(d) The boyhood of Jesus (Luke 2.41-52)

Jewish men were expected to attend the Feasts of Passover, Pentecost and Tabernacles (Booths) if they lived within travelling distance of Jerusalem. Nazareth was ninety miles away, a long distance in those days, but apparently Mary and Joseph were in the habit of going to Jerusalem for the Feast of the Passover every year. When Jesus was twelve he accompanied them. At that age a Jewish boy began to assume the responsibilities and privileges of an adult. T! temple courts were used as places of instruction by learned rabbis, and Jesus may have forgotten the time for their departure in listening to the teachers of his people. Bystanders were impressed by the perception and understanding revealed in the questions he had asked. When Mary scolded him for causing anxiety, Jesus replied in surprise: 'Did you not know that I must be in my Father's house?'

It was unusual for Jews to address God as Father: Jesus must have been aware already of the loving, personal companionship with God into which he was later to draw others. His concern for his 'Father's house' suggests that he had, even then, a sense of commitment to God's service.

(e) Family tree (Luke 3.23-38)

Luke's version of the genealogy of Jesus begins with Joseph and works back through the generations. The names that are mentioned are taken from Hebrew history: it is not an actual family tree so much as a portrayal of Jesus as a representative Jew. Even though he is 'Son of the Most High' and 'Saviour' and 'the Lord's Christ' (1.32; 2.11), he is also a man like other men with a human ancestry.

Luke has a further purpose besides demonstrating Jesus' humanity. To him Jesus is not merely messiah of Israel and son of David; he is God's revelation to the Gentile nations too. And so Luke symbolizes this involvement with all humanity by tracing the ancestry back through David and Abraham to Adam, the mythological first ancestor of the human race. Jesus Christ is son of mankind as well as 'Son of God'.

5. Matthew's Birth and Infancy Narrative
Matt. 1-2

(a) The genealogy of Jesus Christ (Matt. 1.1-17)
Matthew's purpose in writing his gospel is summed up in the opening words. Descended from Judah's Davidic kings and also from the remote ancestor of the Semitic peoples, Abraham, 'father of the faithful', the one of whom he writes fulfils all the expectations and hopes of the Hebrew nation.

Like Luke's, Matthew's genealogy implies belief in the virgin birth: '... Joseph the husband of Mary, of whom Jesus was born, who is called the Christ' (v.16).

Again like Luke, Matthew has not attempted to give an accurate list of Joseph's forbears. Verse 17 is evidence that nothing more than a stylized family tree is intended, and in any case there are too few names to cover all the generations through some 1,700 years.

As Mary's husband, Joseph was legally responsible for her child, even to sharing his ancestry with the boy.

(b) The birth of Jesus (Matt. 1.18-25)
Matthew's birth narrative begins at the point where Joseph learns that Mary is having a baby; there is nothing about Gabriel's visits, Mary's visit to Elizabeth, or John's birth in the Gospel according to Matthew.

According to accepted custom, Joseph should have broken the betrothal contract, but for Mary's sake he intended to do it privately, that is, before three rabbi witnesses. However, before he took any action he had a dream which reassured him that Mary's child was conceived by the Holy Spirit of God. He knew that he should marry Mary and take care of her and her baby. In this account it

139

is Joseph, not Mary, who is told to name the child Jesus.

To Matthew, this birth is a fulfilment of a prophecy in Isaiah 7.14, which he quotes. But the original Hebrew says 'a young girl' and not specifically 'a virgin' shall conceive the child whose name was to be Emmanuel (= God is with us). The early Christians believed that God was indeed with them through Jesus Christ, and so they thought that Isaiah's prophecy of the birth of the child Emmanuel must refer to his birth. The Greek translation of the Hebrew scriptures had used for 'a young girl' a word which also means 'virgin'; it is this translation which Matthew quotes from.

Matthew does not mention Nazareth as being Mary's village and, as we have already noted, does not recount the story of Gabriel's message. Matthew and Luke both say (a) Mary's child was 'of the Holy Spirit' (Matt. 1.20; Luke 1.35); (b) she was betrothed to Joseph but they did not live together until after the baby's birth (Matt. 1.25; Luke 2.5); (c) the baby was born in Bethlehem in the time of Herod the Great (Matt. 2.1; Luke 1.5); and (d) was brought up in Nazareth (Matt. 2.23; Luke 2.39). They differ as to when the boy was taken to Nazareth: Luke says it was straight after the presentation in the temple while Matthew says it was after the family's return from Egypt.

(c) The visit of the wise men (Matt. 2.1-12)

In ancient times stars were associated with the birth of human beings, and any unusual heavenly phenomenon was believed to herald the birth of one who would have great influence in the world. Whatever the actual events which lie behind this story which Matthew alone reports, its value lies in the symbolic offering of worship, wisdom, and wealth to the Jewish Christ by the Gentile world.

The prophet Micah had said that 'one who is to be ruler in Israel, whose origin is from of old, from ancient days', would be born in Bethlehem.[3] Herod wanted no rival claimant to his throne; he secretly intended to murder the child once the wise men had found him.

(d) Egypt and return (Matt. 2.13-23)

Joseph also had a dream which warned him of danger to Jesus.

[3] Micah 5.2-4.

He fled with Mary and the baby by night, and they found refuge in Egypt where there was a colony of Jews. The little family remained there until Joseph received news of Herod's death. On their return, Joseph learnt that Herod's equally cruel son Archelaus ruled Judea, and he travelled on to Galilee and settled in the village of Nazareth. In this way Matthew accounts for the fact that Jesus was known as a Nazarene.

The barbarous Herod had had all the male children under two years of age in Bethlehem slain. Matthew's is the only report we have of such a massacre, but it is consistent with Herod's reputation for insane cruelty.

Luke does not report the visit of the wise men (note that this is how they are described, and the number is not mentioned), nor the murder of the children, nor the flight of Joseph, Mary and Jesus to Egypt.

The importance for Matthew of the Egypt-incident lies in its apparent fulfilment of the words in Hosea: '... and out of Egypt I called my son'.[4] The first Christians were, of course, Jews. They liked to associate Jesus' death with the 'exodus' of their ancestors from slavery in Egypt, the historical events which above all others had convinced them of God's concern for their welfare.

Then Yahweh had welded the tribesmen into Israel, 'my firstborn son', a nation able to take possession of the promised land of Canaan; now his new Israel had been delivered from slavery to sin and given the hope of eternal life through his son Jesus.

(e) The question of the date of Jesus' birth

Herod the Great died in 4 BC. The fact that he killed children up to two years old suggests that the star had appeared not later than 6 BC. (That is, at least two years before his death, though it could have been earlier.)

The Roman census was held at intervals of fourteen years. We know that there was one in AD 6. The one previous to that would therefore have begun in 8 BC. It would have taken some time to reach Judea.

Early in the seventeenth century the astronomer Kepler calculated that there had been an unusual conjunction of the planets Saturn, Jupiter and Mars in the year 7 BC, and that it would have

[4] Hos. 11.1. See also Ex. 4.22.

been visible three times during the year. This particular conjunction of planets occurs only every 800 years. The brightness would have been sufficient to convince astrologers of the birth of a remarkable person.

The evidence we have points to a date for Jesus' birth between 8 and 6 BC, and most probably to 7 BC. How it has come about that he was born BC and not, as one would expect, in AD 1 'the first year of the Lord' is explained in chapter 1.2.

21 *Christ in the Church*

Mark began his gospel with the words: 'The beginning of the gospel of Jesus Christ, the Son of God' because this was the conviction of the church in his day.[1] We have now seen that Matthew and Luke used their birth and childhood stories to state that messiahship and sonship had belonged to Jesus from the very beginning.

Out of this certainty, that God had made himself known in the human life of Jesus of Nazareth, the Christian religion has grown. As the vehicle of divine self-revelation human existence took on new value and significance. Each individual life was seen to have meaning and dignity now that the potential of which human nature was capable was revealed in the life and teaching of the Son of man. God's vindication of the way in which Jesus had lived and died, shown by the resurrection, was assurance that the world is such that love, and the self-giving which stems from love, is the most powerful force in it and will ultimately triumph over hatred and the pursuit of self-interest. This faith gave enormous vitality to the church which sprang into being as a response to the challenge which the life of Christ posed to every man and woman. With it the first Christians believed they could transform the world.

Within a generation or so of Jesus' death it had spread throughout the Roman Empire, not without opposition which flared at times into active persecution, nor the tensions and growing pains

---

[1] Since not all of the earliest manuscripts include the words 'the Son of God' we cannot be certain that Mark wrote them, but they were inserted at an early date, and copied by subsequent scribes, because they expressed the generally held belief. It is quite likely, however, that Mark did write them, because he ends his gospel with the centurion's assertion: 'Truly this man was the (or a) Son of God' (Mark 15.39) and it is the assumption underlying the whole gospel; what more likely than that he also began with this assertion?

which were inevitable as it was lived out in day to day relationships in a different cultural environment. The letters of Paul and the other writings in the New Testament give us a picture of the struggles of this period.

With the conversion of the Emperor Constantine in the fourth century it became the state religion and, while persecution ceased, other problems arose once it was 'respectable' and even desirable to embrace Christianity. The majority of those calling themselves Christians no longer had the sense of dedication and commitment to God, nor the conviction of a living relationship with the Lord Jesus which had transfigured the lives of his first followers. Today its adherents number some hundreds of millions, drawn from every race and cultural background.

Christianity has not always been faithful to the ideals of its founder and for most of its history the Christian church has been unrecognizable as the body of followers of one who taught love and service of others, and who himself lived a life of such simplicity that at times he had nowhere to lay his head and only the lonely hills in which to worship God. Nevertheless it seems to have within itself the seeds of renewal. In its darkest hours fresh movements of the spirit of the living Christ call to repentance and new life.

Despite the unfaithfulness and lukewarmness of many who claim his name, and parodies of his life and teaching which hide him from view, the risen Christ lives on in his church.

INDEX OF PARABLES

INDEX OF MIRACLES

INDEX OF BIBLICAL REFERENCES

GENERAL INDEX

References which are easily found in the contents pages or in the other indexes are not repeated here